australian bush
cooking

easy and tempting recipes for the outdoors

cathy savage & craig lewis

Boiling Billy Publications
www.boilingbilly.com.au

Australian Bush Cooking
is published by
Boiling Billy Publications
Locked Bag 1
Wyndham NSW 2550
Ph/Fax: 02/6494 2727
E-mail: info@boilingbilly.com.au
Web: www.boilingbilly.com.au

design and typesetting by
Craig Lewis/Boiling Billy Design Studio

printed in Australia for the publisher by
Southwood Press
76-82 Chapel St Marrickville NSW 2204

This second edition 2006

ISBN 1 876296 31 3

Whilst all care has been taken by the authors and publisher to ensure that the information contained in this cook book is accurate and up-to-date, the authors nor the publisher can not take any responsibility for the information contained herein. If you come across any shortcomings in this book please write and let us know so we can update in subsequent editions.

To find out more about Boiling Billy Publications and their extensive range of outdoor guides, including their range of best selling camping and 4WD touring books, please visit the website at **www.boilingbilly.com.au**

contents

about the authors

Cathy Savage and Craig Lewis established Boiling Billy Publications in 1995 to write and publish accurate and up-to-date guidebooks for people who love travelling and exploring the wild and remote places of Australia. They have travelled extensively throughout Australia on writing assignments, including an 18 month, 100 000km four-wheel drive odyssey and have been fortunate to have experienced some of the very best that is on offer across this vast country.

As full-time adventurers/authors/publishers they generally camp out around 100 nights each year as part of their extensive field research program. When not on the road travelling they throw down their swag in secluded isolation on the New South Wales Far South Coast.

Their website is at www.boilingbilly.com.au

introduction

Bush cooking these days has well and truly changed from our early settlers cooking. As well as the changes to equipment and utensils, food has changed.

Some people are under the impression that bush cooking only involves camp oven cooking…not necessarily so. Yes, it's true that the camp oven's versatility makes it a great cooking utensil, however there's also the good ol' BBQ plate and grill, the ever faithful frying pan and saucepan and now you can purchase portable smokers, folding ovens and portable spits.

As tastes have changed over time, cooking in the bush is no longer just damper made from water and flour accompanied by a rabbit or kangaroo stew. With Australia's wonderful multiculturalism and diverse eating tastes you can cook just about any of the meals you enjoy cooking at home and even some of those that you go out for.

Even the most patriotic Australian can tire of a BBQ every night, so you'll find recipes in this book using a number of different cooking methods. There is a good mix of BBQ and grilling, pan frying and camp oven cooking. You can even consolidate some meals using the camp oven instead of a frying pan, therefore saving space in your car.

Camping trips are also the cook's holiday, so it's best to work on the 'keep it simple' system. All the recipes included in *Australian Bush Cooking* are based on good eating as well as their ease to prepare and cook and all have been successfully cooked in the bush. Some recipes will require a little more time to prepare and cook than others. Some will be best cooked when you have a standing camp for a day or so, others are nice and easy for when you are overnighting while 'On the Wallaby'. These are recipes that have been collected over the years, some handed down from family and friends.

"Even the most patriotic Australian can tire of a BBQ every night..."

Menu planning is essential by all bush cooks. This is important so that nobody misses out on their favourite meal! Some people might find meal planning a little too predictable, however, if you have a basic menu planned you can swap and change meals around so that when you get to camp you will at least know what to pull out of your tuckerbox. Don't forget to plan for your breakfasts, lunches and inbetween meals snacks!

When planning your menu remember to take into consideration where you will be travelling to, the time spent away from civilisation and shops, and if and when you will be travelling through fruit fly zones. You don't want to throw away any valuable fresh fruit and vegies.

The recipes in this cook book use ingredients that are readily available Australia wide therefore creating no problems with restocking your supplies whilst travelling.

A good idea is to go for a wander down your local supermarket aisles to see what options are available for the bush cook. With food manufacturers so readily aware of everyone's need to save time when cooking there is a great amount of easy to prepare meals that can be utilised in the bush kitchen. As well, most of them are easy to pack and carry.

A good stash of herbs and spices is paramount. Not only are they easy to carry but you can change the taste of a meal with a sprinkle of your favourite herbs or seasoning.

Don't forget when planning your meals to include recipes that can be prepared and cooked by the other half and/or the children. Believe me, there are times when the bush cook needs a rest from the fire.

Along with the range of recipes you will also find inside this book some hints on packing before you go, the pros and cons of car fridges and eskies, details about cryovac meat, suggested items for your tuckerbox and suggested camp cooking equipment. There is also detailed information on the different types of cooking equipment available.

Remember, the secret to a happy bush cook is organisation and preparation. So on arrival to your camp it's well worth your time to arrange for the cooking fire to be started and then all other jobs can follow.

Happy bush cooking — bon appetit.

for safety's sake

Although the majority of the recipes in this book have been designed to be cooked on an open fire using a range of bush cooking utensils, there will be times throughout your travels in the bush that, for any number of reasons, it won't be possible to have a cooking fire.

Circumstances such as days of total fire ban or high fire danger, wet weather or campsites where open fires are not permitted will require the bush cook to plan meals that either do not require cooking or can be cooked on gas appliances.

Please be aware that on days of total fire ban no naked flame is allowed in the open or in canvas (material) tents or camping trailers. This includes liquid fuel and solid fuel stoves (including heat beads), cookers and barbecues.

Be sure to heed warning signs — otherwise it could cost you dearly.

Even on days of high fire danger it may be more prudent to use a gas/fuel stove for cooking instead of an open fire. Please use common sense in these circumstances as carelessness can lead to bushfires, causing destruction to forests and native animals as well as having the potential to threaten human lives and property. Fire restrictions are usually broadcast on local radio stations.

When constructing a cooking fire use an existing fireplace if possible and make sure that all flammable material is cleared at least three metres from around the fire. It is also a good idea to keep some water handy in case of emergency.

Camp fires also have the potential to cause burns. Always use sturdy leather gloves when handling utensils on or near an open fire and if you are using camp ovens a camp oven lifter is essential. These are available from camping and outdoor stores or you can easily make your own from steel rod.

Always carry a well stocked first aid kit and know how to use it.

BEFORE YOU GO

Getting ready can be half the fun. Here's the good oil on planning and preparing for your bush cooking adventures.

planning and packing

Planning and packing for any trip is largely an individual matter, with the amount of time spent on preparation and packing being dependent on the length of your holiday, the areas where you will be travelling to and the amount of space available for packing. Caravanners and long term travellers, for example, will have different requirements than weekend campers.

Start by looking at your trip itinerary and then making a menu prior to leaving. This way you can work out what needs to be purchased before heading off and when and where you can restock your supplies. Also, when you have a menu planned it is a simple matter of collecting the ingredients for the night's dinner and packing them in an easy to reach position that morning, saving you time that night.

Along with the basic items that make up the bulk of the recipes in this book, there are now many items on the supermarket shelf that can be included in your tuckerbox and utilised along with your recipes. Items such as packet pasta, rice mixes and instant meals are useful additions to your pantry, as well as bread mixes that come with their own yeast sachet. These are ideal to make up in the morning as you can leave them to rise during the day whilst travelling and bake them at camp that night.

When packing ensure that you evenly distribute weight so all boxes are easy to lift and carry. We use sturdy plastic containers to store our food in, a wander around hardware stores or large department stores such as Kmart will reveal a range of containers that will suit your needs. You can also use heavy duty cardboard boxes for packing supplies, these are readily available and usually for free. Cardboard boxes with a lid that fits over the box, such as those used for apples and bananas seem to last the longest. One advantage of cardboard boxes over plastic is that they are easily disposed of when they are emptied, freeing up additional room in your vehicle.

Polystyrene foam boxes with fitted lids that are used to transport broccoli and similar vegetables can be used as coolers.

You will find things much easier if you have a number of boxes set aside for specific items. We have a smoko box which is kept in an easy to reach position so we don't have to unpack the vehicle when we stop for a break or for lunch. This box contains plates, bowls, cutlery, cups, basic cooking utensils, cutting board, tea, coffee, sugar and our favourite spreads ie: honey, vegemite, peanut butter and mustard.

You might also consider separate boxes for cooking utensils, tinned food, fruit and vegies, packet foods and condiments. Depending on your type and length of travel will dictate the number of food boxes you will require.

Where possible we usually purchase our sauces and condiments for travelling in plastic containers, otherwise we transfer the contents from the glass container to spare plastic containers. Plastic film canisters are ideal containers for herbs and spices. We then place the labelled canisters inside an empty ice cream container or similar for easy packing.

If planning to travel on outback roads, which are often corrugated, tinned foods will inevitably rub together, causing the labels to come off. In this situation it's a good idea to write the contents on the top of the can with a permanent marker pen. This saves the hassle of opening four tins of baked beans before you finally find the tin of peeled tomatoes you required for a recipe.

portable fridge or ice box cooler?

Portable fridges have gained in popularity over the last few years and for the serious camper these are a great convenience. Portable fridges are either 'two way'—those that run on both 12 volt DC, such as from your vehicle's battery, and 240 volt AC from a standard power point; or 'three way' fridges which operate on the previous two power sources as well as bottled gas or LPG. Some 'two way' fridges may require an additional transformer to operate on 240 volt DC.

The drawback with portable fridges are their price with quality units ranging in price from between $500 to $1800 or more. In addition, if you are using your vehicle's battery as the fridge's sole power source it is wise to fit a second battery so you won't accidentally be left stranded with a flat battery.

If you only take a few camping holidays each year then hiring a portable fridge may prove to be more economical. Fridges can usually be hired for weekends, weekly hires or longer.

Over the years we have used a number of different 12 volt fridges inlcuding the Australian made *Autofridge* and *EvaKool* as well as a *Waeco*, all of which have been both reliable and efficient during our travels.

The humble ice box cooler or 'esky' has been keeping the beer cold on camping trips for years. Advantages of ice boxes are their cheap purchase price, compared to portable fridges, and their portability, as they don't have to be plugged into a power source they can be placed practically anywhere that is convenient. However, for ice boxes to be effective they need a supply of ice, which may or may not be readily available depending on your type of travel and style of camping. Block ice will keep longer than crushed ice. 'Dry ice' which is solid carbon dioxide, is an alternative to block and crushed ice, however, it is generally only available in cities and some larger centres.

Our 90 litre Evakool fridge

cryovac meat

A real boon for campers is cryovac, a process of packing meat products in heavy duty plastic packaging and then removing all oxygen by a vacuum process. The removal of oxygen helps stop the meat dehydrating and any degradation to the product. Under specific temperature controls the shelf life of meat can be extended anything up to four or more weeks, depending on the type of meat.

Cryovac or vacuum sealing not only prolongs the shelf life of your meat whilst travelling, it will stop any blood leaking into your fridge or esky from your meat packaging.

Obviously whilst travelling and camping using an ice box or esky you do not have as great a control over temperature levels as if you are using a portable fridge, you can still utilise this process and carry enough meat with you to last a week or two before having to search out a butcher.

Time variations also occur depending on the type of meat. Beef will have the longest storage period – approximately 3 to 4 weeks when meat is kept at a constant 1° Celsius; lamb is next – around 2 to 3 weeks; then meat such as pork, chicken and processed meats ie: sausages are best used within the first week.

Things to remember with cryovaced products:

• Meat with a bone can be cryovaced but must have bone guards.

• Do not have meat that has fresh additives – ie: herbs, spices, vegetables or fruit cryovaced. If you are buying herbed or spicy sausages ensure that the butcher has used dried and sanitized ingredients, such as those done by companies like Masterfoods etc.

• Dark cut meat should not be cryovaced. Use the freshest meat possible.

• Use punctured packages first. It is an idea to always inspect meat packages each night to look for any wear or rub marks on your packages.

• Cryovac meat can be frozen then placed in your fridge or esky to defrost slowly. By freezing the meat this will add some extra shelf life to your meat.

• Once opened the meat can have a slight confinement odour, this odour is just the mixture of the meat scent and carbon dioxide – the meat is okay to eat and the odour will dissipate after about five minutes.

When we travel we usually work out our menu in two week segments and have our local butcher cryovac enough meat to last us the two weeks, this includes bacon for breakfasts and meat for our evening meals including chicken breasts, mixed grills and other cuts of meat. Therefore we don't need to shop until the end of our second week. All we may need is either a small general store or service station to top up bread and milk. However, we always leave a nice piece of fillet steak cryovacced for about 4 to 5 weeks, the meat is simply divine and extremely tender when barbecued.

For further information about the cryovac process have a chat with your local butcher and discuss your camping and travelling requirements with them. They'll advise you on the best cuts to cryovac and their approximate keeping times.

cooking with gas

On all your trips to the bush it is a good idea to carry some type of liquid fuel stove to use when the weather prevents cooking over a fire or restrictions do not allow fires. For example, many national park and state forest camping areas in South Australia and some Murray River and Murrumbidgee River forests in New South Wales have solid fuel fire bans over the summer fire danger period, making a liquid fuel stove essential in these areas. Camping areas in other states also have solid fuel fire bans. Solid fuel fires include fires that are made from wood and/or heat bead products.

Gas stoves are essential for times when fires are not allowed or impractical.

Please remember that on days of total fire ban that the use of liquid fuel stoves, cookers and barbecues in the open are also prohibited.

There is a vast array of stoves on the market burning fuels such as unleaded petrol, butane gas through to methylated spirits. However, the most common type of fuel stove burns liquid petroleum gas, or LPG, which is readily available in refillable bottles.

Single ring burners that screw directly to the top of gas bottles are great for a quick cuppa or one pot meals, however the two and three burner free standing stoves tend to be more practical if cooking for more than a couple of people. Cast iron gas burner rings are another alternative.

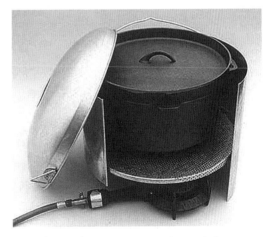

Gas conversion for camp ovens.

Many of the recipes in this book can easily be cooked on a gas stove, even those involving camp ovens can be cooked by using a number of gas conversion attachments for camp ovens. These units, such as the Australian made *Camp Oven Mate* from Southern Metal Spinners (pictured left) or the *Gas Conversion Kit* by Hillbilly Camping Gear allow you to cook your favourite camp oven meals without the aid of coals from a fire. Ideal in national parks that do not allow solid fuel fires.

Carrying water

Water is one of the most important but often rarely considered necessities for the bush cook. Good clean water is essential for both drinking and cooking.

It is getting steadily more difficult to rely on water from streams and rivers in the bush to provide safe, uncontaminated drinking water so it is best to carry your own from a known, reliable source.

Carry water in containers that have been designed for that purpose and have not previously contained any other liquid that could contaminate or taint the water. It is safest to carry water in at least two separate containers. If one splits or springs a leak you won't lose all your valuable water.

What rubbish!

It's a simple rule when it comes to rubbish—if you can carry it in, you can carry it out. It is okay to burn paper and cardboard packaging in your fire, however, take everything else with you. We use plastic shopping bags for our rubbish which we then place in heavy duty garbage bags with draw top closures which are taken to the nearest rubbish disposal centre.

Never bury rubbish as it is likely to be dug up by animals.

the tuckerbox

Your menu requirements and the length of your trip will determine what food you pack and take with you. Here are a few suggestions.

tinned foods

* Tomatoes
* Tomato puree
* Corn kernels
* Sweet and sour sauce
* Baked beans
* Spaghetti
* 4 bean mix
* Soups
* Capsicum
* Chinese vegetables
* Mushrooms
* Sliced beetroot
* Tuna
* Ham
* Pineapple pieces
* Fruits
* Carrots
* Peas
* Smoked oysters

packet foods

- Long life milk
- Long life custard
- Long life cream
- Milk powder
- Custard powder
- Tomato paste sachets
- Cornflour
- Self-raising flour
- Plain flour
- Baking powder
- Pasta
- Instant pasta mixes
- Instant rice mixes
- Instant meal mixes
- Rice
- Cereals
- Dried peas
- Dried beans
- French onion soup mix
- Other soup mixes
- Instant noodles
- Biscuits, plain, sweet and crackers
- Dried fruits
- Marshmallows

herbs and spices

- Mixed herbs
- Steak spice
- Ground coriander
- Chinese five spice
- Curry powder
- Chilli powder
- Ground ginger
- Cinnamon sugar
- Garlic granules
- Onion flakes
- Mustard powder
- Cajun spice
- Cayenne pepper
- Lemon pepper

condiments

- Oil
- Tomato sauce
- BBQ sauce
- Worcestershire sauce
- Satay sauce
- Soy sauce
- Salt & pepper
- Stock cubes: beef, chicken and vegetable
- Mustard
- Chutney

fruit and vegetables

Prior to purchasing and packing fruit and vegetables check against your itinerary when and if you will be passing through fruit fly zones. It is best to leave purchasing these items until after you have travelled through the fruit fly exclusion zones otherwise they will need to be discarded at roadside disposal areas.

Fruit and vegetables will travel well outside a fridge or ice box, however it is best if you wrap each item individually in newspaper or butchers paper to protect them. Also, by doing this if one spoils it won't affect all of your supplies. Good travellers include:

- Potatoes
- Onions
- Pumpkin
- Sweet Potatoes
- Carrots
- Cabbage
- Zucchini
- Broccoli
- Capsicum
- Cucumber
- Tomatoes
- Apples
- Oranges
- Mandarins
- Melons
- Bananas

BUSH COOKING EQUIPMENT

From Barbecues to Billies and Tripods to Trivets, cooking in a bush kitchen is a whole lot easier with the right gear.

camp ovens

Camp ovens are one of the most useful, yet to many, most daunting pieces of bush cooking equipment. However, with a little practice the art of cooking in a camp oven will become rewarding as well as enjoyable.

There are two types of camp ovens readily available, cast iron and spun steel.

A - Cast Iron: These are the most common type of ovens available, ranging from low priced imported ovens through to the top quality *Furphy Foundry* ovens.

The advantages of cast iron camp ovens is their ability to hold an even heat for considerable periods, which is important when cooking on coals. Their main drawback is their weight. Also, there is a tendency for cast iron ovens to crack or shatter if dropped or stored incorrectly when travelling. This is more so with the cheaper imported ovens that are generally not as heavy duty.

B - Spun Steel: The traditional Bedourie style oven (B - bottom of picture) can be used as an oven and in addition the lid turned upside down used as a frying pan. Advantages of Bedourie ovens are that they are lightweight and compact, making them easy to pack. Care is required with the amount of heat when using a Bedourie oven, especially when roasting and baking. Spun steel, being thinner than cast iron, transfers heat quickly and more intensley, which can result in burnt offerings if careful attention is not payed when cooking. The Bedourie oven originated from the Bedourie district in western Queensland and it is said that this type of camp oven became popular with drovers due to its lightweight and robustness compared to the more fragile and heavier cast iron ovens.

Spun steel camp ovens are also available in the traditional shape (B - top of picture) similar to cast iron ovens. These ovens, made by *Hillbilly Camping Gear*, are quite deep with a large dished lid to hold coals. Concentrating the heat on the lid helps avoid sticking and burning the food on the base of the camp oven.

barbecues and grills

Barbecues and grills/grates are available in a huge range of sizes and styles with most camping and outdoor stores having a large selection to choose from.

When selecting a portable barbecue you will find the types with folding or removable legs much more convenient to pack in your vehicle. Also, many of the portable barbecues now available have both a steel plate as well as a grate section which many people find more versatile than a barbecue that is all plate.

C - Circular steel plate barbecue: This style of barbecue is based on the old plough disk barbecue plate of rural Australia. The barbecue pictured is a *Biji Barbi* and consists of a round steel plate with a slight dish to allow the fat and oil to run to the centre and drip through a small hole, adding fuel to your cooking fire. There are three folding legs as well as a folding handle. We have found this to be an excellent product and is a permanent piece of our cooking gear.

D - Swinging grill: Lightweight stainless steel grill, by *Carr-B-Que,* is both simple to use and easy to carry. Cooks everything from steak, chops, snags to toast to even boiling the billy!

E - Swinging barbecue plate: This style of barbecue consists of a steel rod hammered into the ground with the barbecue plate swinging on a neck. The unit pictured is manufactured by *Hillbilly Camping Gear.* A disadvantage with this type of setup, as with the swinging grill above, is that they are not suitable for very rocky or hard surfaces.

F - Folding grate and barbecue plate: A simple folding grate is a useful addition to your bush cooking gear. The one pictured was homemade by Craig from an old wire fridge shelf reinforced with a welded steel frame. The legs are made from steel rod. A rectangular steel barbecue plate with a handle sits on top when required.

Similar grates are available at outdoor and camping stores or if you are handy you might like to make one. Alternatively, your local engineering/welding shop could make one for you.

pots and pans

A frying pan and a couple of pots or saucepans are valuable additions to your bush cooking gear. These items allow greater scope to your bush culinary delights, especially for long term travellers and campers where a camp oven and barbie just won't do the job.

G - Spun steel frying pan: This large spun steel frying pan from *Hillbilly Camping Gear* swings on a steel spike allowing it to be adjusted above the fire. It can also be swung away from the fire when turning food. The steel spike also holds the swinging barbecue plate.

H - Cast iron frying pan: Heavyweight cast iron frying pan.

I - Cast iron saucepan: Cast iron saucepans retain an even heat over an open fire but are heavy, and like cast iron camp ovens and frying pans require careful packing and transporting.

smokers

Portable smoke ovens provide a tasty alternative to traditional cooking styles such as barbecuing and roasting. Just sprinkle a little sawdust in the bottom of the smoker, place your food on the rack, light the methylated spirit burner and your smoking!

J - Circular stainless steel smoker: This large circular smoke oven manufactured by *Togar Ovens* has enough room to smoke anything from fish to chicken.

K - Galvanised smoker box: Again can be used to smoke a variety of foods. *Nipper Kipper Smoke Ovens* come in galvanised iron or stainless steel, and have developed an oven that folds for easy carrying.

billies and kettles

Billies and kettles are indispensable to the bush cook. In its simplest form a *billy* is a tin can with a wire handle usually used to boil water over an open fire for a cup of tea. There is much conjecture to the origin of the term billy. One theory is that it

came from the French word *bouilli*, which was a tinned French soup eaten by diggers on the early goldfields. The empty tin was then used to boil water for tea. Another explanation is that the word originated from the scottish *'bally'*, which means milk pail.

L - Aluminium billy: Lightweight, no-rust billy based on the original, no-frills design. Also available with a spout (as pictured) for easy pouring.

M - Tin billy: Tin billies have a tendency to rust if not dried properly after use.

N - Enamel coffee pot style kettle: We find this type of kettle easy to use due to its spout and handle for easy pouring and close fitting lid.

O - Eco Billy: The kettle pictured is an *Eco Billy*. These are great for a quick lunch time cuppa when you are on the move. Simply fill the billy with water, grab a handful of leaves, bark and twigs and set these alight. The billy is cyclindrical so the fire burns up through the centre of the billy. All you do is feed a few small twigs through the centre chimney and the water for your brew will be boiled in no time.

spits

P - Portable Spits: The two portable spits pictured will add a difference to your camp kitchen and make a great alternative to the camp oven roast. Both come with a spit motor which is run by 2 'D' batteries.

The *Auspit* (P rear) is designed for use over an open fire and has height adjustment and a swing away action. This lightweight unit comes in its own carry bag.

The *Aussie Porta Spit* (P front) comes complete with its own fire bin.

accessories

These camp oven accessories make handling the oven easier and enhances the camp ovens cooking ability.

Q - Camp oven lifters: Camp oven lifters are the most convenient way of moving hot camp ovens around and lifting coal laden camp oven lids. The pair pictured right are made by *Eco Billy/Murray River Innovations*.

R - Oven trivet: Place the trivet in the base of the camp oven to use as a platform to put food on. Pictured is a trivet manufactured by *Hillbilly Camping Gear* (R left) to suit their ovens and one that we purchased from a kitchenware shop (R right).

S - Vegie Ring: This *Hillybilly Camping Gear* vegie ring is designed to sit in the top of the camp oven so vegies can be roasted whilst the meat is in the base of the camp oven.

T - Pot stand: This pot stand manufactured by *Hillybilly Camping Gear* is designed to sit on the lid of the camp oven so cooking can be done in a frying pan or saucepan whilst roasting or baking, utilising the heat on the lid of the camp oven.

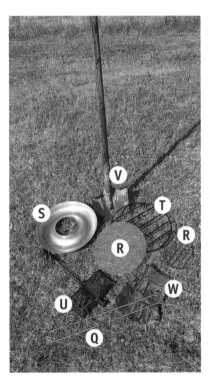

U - Jaffle iron: A cast iron jaffle iron is an ideal item to have in your camp kitchen kit. Perfect for toasted sandwiches, savoury or sweet. Just place the jaffle iron on top of some hot coals, turn it over regularly to ensure even cooking and you have a perfect toasted sandwich.

V - Shovel: A shovel is essential for moving coals around your bush kitchen. You will require a shovel to place coals on the lids of camp ovens; move coals away from the main fire for simmering; dig a trench for a pit fire plus numerous other uses. If you have the room, such as a roof rack or trailer then a long handle shovel is the preferred type for bush kitchens, however any type of shovel will do the job. The great thing about long handle shovels is that you can gather cooking coals for your camp oven without getting too close to the heat of the main fire.

W - Leather Gloves: A pair, or preferably two, of sturdy leather gloves makes handling cooking equipment much safer and helps prevent burns and scalds.

care of cast iron and spun steel cookware

Cast iron and spun steel cookware, whether they be camp ovens, frying pans or saucepans, require special attention after use to prevent rust and corrosion forming, and shortening the life of the utensil.

To clean an oven or pan warm it near the fire to loosen food particles, fat and oils then wipe out the oven or pan with paper towel or similar. This will leave a coating of oil on the inside of the oven or pan which will prevent it from rusting. For long term storage between trips throughly wash the oven or pan in hot soapy water and allow to dry, preferably near the fire or stove top. When completely dry wipe the inside of the utensil with cooking oil to prevent rust.

suggested equipment

cooking equipment

- Matches
- Firelighters
- A two burner gas stove and gas bottle
- BBQ plate
- Grill or grate – excellent for placing frying pans, saucepans and camp ovens on over the fire
- 2 x saucepans with lids
- Frying pan
- Camp ovens – 2 if you have room
- Trivet – to use inside the camp oven to place dishes on

- 2 x Billies
- Tripod hanger
- Spit (if spit roasting)
- Pie dish – to fit camp oven
- Loaf tin – to fit camp oven
- Pizza tray – to fit camp oven
- Camp oven lid lifters – to help lift camp ovens out of coals and also to take the lid off the camp oven
- Shovel - preferably long handled
- 2 pairs of thick leather gloves

Cooking Utensils

- Mixing bowls – we use empty ice cream containers with lids. These can be used for serving and also for storage.

- Small measuring jug

- Tongs – short or long

- Bar-B-Q Mate

- Basting brush

- Serving spoon

- Slotted serving spoon

- Peelers

- Egg flip

- Flat grater

- Can opener with bottle opener

- Swiss army knife – with cork screw

- Flat strainer

- Egg rings

- 1 large sharp knife

- 1 bread knife

- Cutting board

- Mesh toaster

- General purpose scissors

- Measuring spoon or a tablespoon

- Extra plate and bowl for serving

- Teaspoons

personal eating equipment

- Plate
- Bowl
- Mug
- Fork
- Spoon
- Knife
- Steak Knife

miscellaneous items

- Roll of aluminium foil
- Roll of cling wrap
- Paper towel
- Plastic bottle for milk
- Plastic bottle for cordial
- Plastic bottle for extra water

cleaning equipment

- Plastic bags
- Wash up bucket
- Container of detergent
- Scourer – the non scratch ones are good

- Cloths
- Dish brush
- Tea towels

cooking fires and coals

making your cooking fire

You can build an above ground fire, and as the name suggests these sit on the ground, or you can dig a trench or pit for a pit fire. Pit fires have some advantages over above ground fires such as not being effected as much by wind, making them safer in windy conditions and also they tend to radiate heat better—especially if using poor quality wood. However, it may be difficult or near impossible to dig a pit or trench if your fire is situated on hard, rocky ground. Either way you should clear the area of combustible material such as leaves, dried grass and twigs for at least three metres around your fire site.

Get your cooking fire going well before it is time to start cooking.

Some people place rocks around the perimeter of the fire to act as a barrier. If you do this, *never* use rounded river stones. These nearly always explode, sending razor sharp fragments of rock flying in all directions when subjected to the intense heat of a camp fire.

Another point worth remembering is that many campsites, and especially the more popular ones, are usually devoid of wood for a fire. It is best to collect a good supply of firewood well before reaching your campsite or if you have room bring some from home.

Try to avoid collecting logs that are hollow as these are often home to small animals and lizards. *Never* cut down trees, either living or dead — always collect fallen wood for your fire.

Heavy, dense hardwoods such as red gum, ironbark, blue gum, stringy-bark and similar eucalyptus are slow burning and will produce good cooking coals. In the western and outback areas mulga, gidgee and desert oak produce excellent coals. Gidgee and red gum are favourites of ours as they produce reliable coals for cooking.

Softwoods like pine aren't suitable for cooking fires as they do not produce very good coals, mostly burning to ash.

It's a handy idea to take along a packet of commercial firelighters which you can get at supermarkets. These make lighting a fire much easier than using paper, especially when the wood is damp. *Never* use petrol to light a fire.

getting ready to cook

It is best to start your fire at least 30 minutes, or better still, an hour or so prior to cooking. You will find that the best cooking fire is one with low flame and plenty of glowing coals and this takes time. You can't build a good cooking fire in ten minutes!

For most camp oven cooking you will need a main fire from which to produce coals and a level area a short distance away from this for your coal bed. Some people place aluminium foil on the ground before placing the coals on the coal bed near the main fire. This helps to reduce heat loss from the coals on the cold ground. If you are using a trench fire move the required amount of coals to one end of the trench. If you are barbecuing, grilling or frying wait until the main fire has produced a good bed of coals and place your grate or plate directly over these.

The different cooking styles will use different parts of the fire:
• Barbecuing, boiling and frying – over direct flame
• Roasting, stewing and grilling – use red embers and coals
• Coal cooking – use grey embers. Wrap food in aluminium foil and bury in the grey embers.

For hints on successful cooking in your camp oven see *Using your Camp Oven* on page 51.

windy weather

Wind can be a real nuisance for the bush cook. Besides blowing dust and grit around and covering everything you cook on the fire with ash, strong winds also make it more difficult to control the heat of your cooking fire by fanning the coals and creating 'hot spots'.

When setting up your bush kitchen take note of the prevailing wind if there is any and use any natural protection such as trees and large boulders if possible. At times you may need to use your food boxes or whatever is available to form a windbreak. A strategically placed vehicle can also act as an effective windbreak. Please do not cut down any living vegetation to use as a windbreak.

BREAKFAST

Breakfast while camping is often a much more leisurely affair than the rushed 'scoff down a bite while rushing out the door' scenario of our working weekdays. These breakfasts are sure to get you off to a great start.

potato omelette

Cooking time: around 30 minutes. Serves 2

Cook bacon in hot oil in frying pan until crisp, remove.

Add potatoes, shallots, herbs and Tabasco to pan. Cook until potatoes are just tender, around 20 minutes, carefully stirring a couple of times.

Add milk to beaten eggs – mix well. Pour eggs and milk over potato mixture. Cover and cook until eggs are set.

Tip ~ Serve sliced with bacon sprinkled on top. This dish is great served at breakfast or even for lunch.

4 bacon rashers, diced
2 medium potatoes, peeled and thinly sliced
4 shallots, sliced
1 tablespoon dried mixed herbs
Tabasco sauce, to taste
4 eggs, beaten
2 tablespoons milk

mud pirate's eggs

Cooking time: 5-10 minutes. Ingredients per person

Butter bread on both sides and cut a hole in the middle. Keep centre. Place bread on barbecue plate or in frying pan.

Break egg into each hole and cook till firm on the bottom. Carefully flip over and cook other side.

Serve with the fried cut out on top of egg.

Tip ~ Serve by themselves or with bacon, sausage and fried mushrooms.

1 egg
1 slice of bread

bushman's toast

Beat eggs and add milk. Dip bread in mixture then fry on both sides until golden brown.

Serve with bacon or with maple syrup.

Tip ~ For a sweeter option use fruit or raisin bread.

2 eggs
3 tablespoons milk
4 slices of bread
Butter for frying

basic pancake mix

Makes 8-10 pancakes.

Combine flour, pinch of salt and egg. Gradually add milk and beat until smooth.

Leave to stand for 1 hour.

Heat frying pan and lightly rub with butter. Pour 2 to 3 tablespoons of batter into frying pan tilting pan until batter is evenly distributed.

Cook until bubbles appear, flip over and cook second side.

Serve with butter and golden or maple syrup; fresh lemon juice and sugar; or our favourite with fresh fruit, yoghurt and golden syrup.

1 cup self raising flour
Pinch of salt
1 egg
1 cup milk

tomato, onion and bacon fry up

Cooking time: around 10 minutes. Serves 3-4

1 onion, sliced
2 bacon rashers, chopped
1x415g tin of tomatoes, chopped
Salt and pepper to taste

Heat oil in frying pan. Fry onion and bacon until just cooked. Add roughly chopped tomatoes and cook until the liquid evaporates. Add two tablespoons of water and fry until liquid evaporates.

Season with salt and pepper. Serve on toast by itself or with egg.

no trouble bubble & squeak

Left over cooked mashed potatoes
Left over cooked vegetables

Mix left over mash and vegetables together. Season with salt and pepper.

Heat oil or butter in frying pan or on barbecue plate. Place vegetable mix in oil and flatten out. Cook until browned then turn over and brown other side. Don't worry if they break up.

Serve with bacon and eggs for a filling breakfast.

mick's mini omelettes

Serves 2-3

4 eggs
½ onion, finely diced
½ capsicum, finely diced
Milk – a few drops per egg
Salt and pepper to taste

Heat barbecue plate or frying pan. Beat together eggs, onion, capsicum, milk and seasoning.

Spoon mixture into greased egg rings. Cook approximately 1 minute – turn and cook other side.

Tip ~ These omelettes are great served with sausages or bacon or wack them on toasted muffins - beautiful.

corn fritters

Serves 2

1x420g canned corn kernels, drained
1 cup plain flour
2 teaspoons baking powder
½ teaspoon salt
2 eggs
Butter

Beat all ingredients, except butter, together.

Heat butter in frying pan or on barbecue plate. Place a few tablespoons of corn mixture onto butter. Fry both sides till golden brown.

Serve at breakfast with bacon and toast.

Tip ~ Self raising flour can be substituted for the plain flour and baking powder.

beardies potato cakes

Serves enough for 4-6 people

Squeeze liquid out of grated potatoes and onion.

Combine all ingredients. Drop small spoonfuls into hot oil on barbecue plate or in frying pan. Cook until well browned on both sides.

Tip ~ These potato cakes are delicious served by themselves or as part of a big breakfast fry up with bacon and eggs. For those who like to turn up the heat a friend of ours serves these with a sliced jalepeno chilli pressed in the middle of the potato cake.

4 potatoes, grated
1 onion, grated
4 tablespoons plain flour
2 eggs
Salt and Pepper to taste

never never corn and bacon pancakes

Cooking time: around 10 minutes. Makes approximately 12-15 pancakes

Lightly fry diced bacon and let cool. Combine flour and pinch of salt in bowl.

Make a well in the flour and add egg. Gradually stir in 1 cup of milk. Mix to a smooth batter.

Add bacon and corn, mix well to a smooth pouring batter. Add extra milk if necessary.

Heat frying pan or barbecue plate and brush with a little butter. Cook thin layers of batter on each side until cooked and golden.

Tip ~ Serve with extra bacon rashers or with golden or maple syrup.

1 cup self-raising flour
Salt
1 egg
1 cup milk
2 bacon rashers, diced
1x300g tin of corn kernels, well drained

sausage and beans breakfast

Cooking time: 30 minutes. Serves 4

Cook sausages in frying pan or on barbecue plate. Drain on paper towels.

Heat oil in frying pan and cook onions until soft. Add tomatoes, baked beans, water and tomato paste. Bring to the boil and simmer for 5 minutes. Stir occasionally to stop sticking, add extra water if necessary.

Return sausages to pan and heat through.

Tip ~ For some extra flavour add a dash of Tabasco or Worcestershire sauce.

Allow 2 thick sausages per person
Oil
2 large onions, chopped
1x420g tin tomatoes, crushed
1x420gm tin baked beans in tomato sauce
½ cup water
2 tablespoons tomato paste

BARBEQUES AND GRILLING

The good ol' barbie is often the basis of most outdoor cooking while camping. These barbecue and grilling recipes are sure to take the humble chops and snags to mouth-watering new heights around the camp fire.

tandoori lamb cutlets

Cooking time: around 10-15 minutes

Mix yoghurt and Tandoori marinade together. Use enough for your tastes, we usually use about half a packet or quarter of a bottle. Add a splash of oil and mix well.

Thoroughly coat lamb cutlets with mix and leave to marinate.

Barbecue cutlets on well oiled barbecue plate or grill over hot coals until cooked.

Serve with green salad or with the couscous salad on page 83.

Lamb cutlets, 2-3 per person depending on size
Small tub of natural yoghurt
Splash of oil
Indian Tandoori Marinade, either sauce or powder

fruity lamb chops

Cooking time: around 20 minutes

Season chops with salt and pepper. Barbecue chops on oiled barbecue plate until tender.

When chops are just tender, place sliced fruit on barbecue plate. Brush fruit with melted butter and sprinkle with cinnamon, cook until tender and slightly browned. Serve chops with fruit on top.

Tip ~ Delicious served with baked potato and salad.

Lamb chops, either loin or forequarter, 1-2 per person
Sliced fruit – either mango or peach (fresh is best – but tinned will do)
Salt and pepper
Melted butter
Ground cinnamon

cobbler lamb chops and red wine

Cooking time: around 15-20 minutes. Serves 4

Cook lamb chops on oiled barbecue or grill.

While chops are cooking, melt butter in a small saucepan, add garlic and vegetables and cook until tender. Add tomato paste, wine and seasonings. Cook until well mixed and heated through.

Serve chops with sauce on top.

8 lamb forequarter chops
1 clove garlic, crushed
2 tablespoons butter
2 carrots, cut into strips
6 mushrooms, sliced
2 onions, chopped
2 tablespoons tomato paste
2 tablespoons red wine
Salt and pepper to taste

chilli pork chops

Cooking time: around 15-20 minutes. Serves 6

6-8 pork chops
Oil
1 large onion, chopped
1 garlic clove, crushed
½ cup chilli sauce
¼ cup beer
Couple splashes of Tabasco sauce

In small saucepan or frying pan cook onion and garlic in hot oil until tender. Add chilli sauce, beer and Tabasco sauce. Bring to the boil and remove from heat.

Barbecue chops on oiled barbecue plate or grill, brushing chops with sauce whilst cooking.

Serve chops with any remaining sauce heated through.

bbq pork spare ribs

Cooking time: around 20 minutes. Serves 4

1kg pork spare ribs
¼ cup oil
1 tablespoon lemon juice
1 tablespoon Worcestershire sauce
1 garlic clove, crushed
1 tablespoon brown sugar
½ teaspoon dry mustard
¼ cup fruit chutney

Combine marinade ingredients and mix well.

Brush mixture all over ribs and let stand for several hours.

Barbecue ribs until golden brown and cooked through, basting with marinade during cooking.

Tip ~ Try one of the other marinades as detailed in the Marinades and Bastes section on page 106.

glazed pork chops

Cooking time: around 15-20 minutes. Serves 4

4 pork chops
⅓ cup apricot jam
1 packet French Onion Soup Mix
Juice of 1 orange

Mix the jam, orange juice and soup mix together. Brush glaze over pork chops.

Cook chops on barbecue plate or grill, brushing with glaze whilst cooking.

Serve glazed chops with green salad.

ABOVE: *Breakfast fry up on the Biji Barbi (page 18) of Mud Pirate's Eggs (page 27), Mick's Mini Omelettes (page 28), Beardies Potato Cakes (page 29), bacon, tomato and toast on the Carr-B-Que (page 18).*

RIGHT: *Boiling the Eco Billy for a morning cuppa (page 20).*

BELOW: *Stuffed Pumpkin cooked in the camp oven (page 69) can be served as a side with roast or barbecued meat or as a meal by itself.*

ABOVE: *A feast of boiled yabbies ready for the recipes on page 48.*

LEFT: *Cath dishing out Cocky's Joy Dumplings from the camp oven (page 88). These dumplings are delicious served with custard and cream.*

BELOW: *Beef Casserole with Doughboy's Dumplings (page 55) is a tasty camp oven meal.*

ABOVE: *Diggers Meat Loaf and salad (page 58). Diggers Meat Loaf also tastes great the next day on sandwiches with your favourite sauce. Make up Diggers Meat Loaf with your choice of vegetables.*

BELOW: *Spit roasting a rolled pork loin (page 73) using the Australian made Aussie Porta Spit (page 20). Spit roasting is a great alternative to roasting in the camp oven.*

ABOVE: *Damper is one of the most popular foods to be cooked in the camp oven. As every bush cook has their own secret recipe, we have supplied a variety of recipes and ideas in section 11 Damper, Bread, Scones and Muffins on page 94.*

BELOW: *BBQ Pork Spare Ribs (page 32) cooked over coals on the Carr-B-Que (page 18).*

bbq corn on the cob

If using fresh corn, remove silks from corn, but leave husks on. Spread butter over corn cob.

Wrap each cob in foil and barbecue for about 30 minutes until tender. Be sure to turn often to avoid burning.

Tip ~ Add one of the following to the butter for additional flavour: crushed garlic, dried herbs, crushed chilli or chilli powder.

Corn cob per person
Butter

backblocks spicy steaks

Cooking time: around 15 minutes. Serves 4

Mix together oil, onion, sauces, lemon juice and paprika. Add meat and marinate for at least one hour prior to cooking.

Brush grill or barbecue plate with oil and cook meat over hot coals, brushing with marinade whilst cooking.

Steak per person
2 tablespoons oil
1 onion, finely chopped
3 tablespoons Worcestershire sauce
2 tablespoons tomato sauce
Juice of 1 lemon
1 tablespoon paprika

ringers steak & onion

Cooking time: around 20 minutes. Serves 4

Combine ¼ cup beer and Worcestershire sauce, brush over steak.

Barbecue steak over hot coals, brushing with sauce whilst cooking. While steaks are cooking you may as well finish off the rest of the beer!

Meanwhile on barbecue plate or in frying pan, melt butter and cook onion, capsicum and garlic until tender.

Serve steak with vegetables on top.

Steak for each person
Can of beer, ¼ cup reserved
2 tablespoons Worcestershire sauce
1 large onion, sliced
1 capsicum, sliced
2 garlic cloves, crushed
Butter

beef, pineapple and capsicum kebabs

Cooking time: around 15 minutes. Serves 3-4

500g rump steak, cubed
1 tin pineapple cubes
1 red capsicum, cubed

MARINADE
1 cup chicken stock
¼ cup honey
⅓ cup tomato sauce
1 garlic clove, crushed
2 tablespoons soy sauce
½ teaspoon chilli powder
Ground black pepper to taste

Alternatively thread beef, pineapple and capsicum onto skewers and place in shallow dish. Combine all marinade ingredients and pour over kebabs. Leave for an hour.

Barbecue on well oiled barbecue plate or grill until cooked. Brush with reserved marinade whilst cooking.

Tip ~ If using bamboo skewers, soak in water for 30 minutes prior to using to stop skewers burning whilst cooking.

chicken satay sticks

Cooking time: around 15 minutes

2 chicken breasts, cut into strips
1 bottle/tin of satay sauce

Thread chicken strips onto skewers (see above tip about skewers). Cook on well oiled barbecue plate or grill.

Brush with satay sauce while cooking.

bbq chicken wings

Cooking time: around 30 minutes

1kg of chicken wings will give you around 12 wings

MARINADE
2 tablespoons each of:
tomato sauce
BBQ sauce
honey
¼ cup white wine (or even beer)
Dash Tabasco sauce

Combine all marinade ingredients. Cover chicken wings with marinade and leave until required, or at least one hour.

Barbecue wings on oiled hotplate or grill until cooked through and well browned.

The wings can be left whole or you can cut them in half at the joint.

Tip ~ For other marinade flavours see the Marinades and Bastes section on page 106.

rissoles

Rissoles would have to be a favourite to have while camping or when having a barbecue. Here we have included a few different flavours for you to try. Rissoles can be served by themselves with salad or vegetables or served on fresh bread or buns as burgers with salad and your favourite sauce. After shaping your rissoles it is best for them to be refrigerated for a while prior to cooking. These rissoles can also be cooked in a frying pan over good heat.

herbed beef rissoles

Cooking time: around 15 minutes. This recipe makes 6 large rissoles

Mix all ingredients together thoroughly and divide into 6 equal size rissoles. Refrigerate if possible until ready to cook.

Cook rissoles on lightly oiled barbecue plate.

1kg beef mince
1 teaspoon of each:
dried thyme
dried rosemary
dried basil
¼ cup sour cream

baitlayers rissoles

Cooking time: around 15 minutes. Makes 6 rissoles

Combine mince, breadcrumbs, egg and Tabasco sauce together and form into 6 rissoles.

Make a hole in each rissole with your finger and place an oyster inside. Cover with mince.

Cook rissoles on lightly oiled barbecue plate.

Tip ~ For a change place a chunk of your favourite cheese inside the rissole instead of the oyster.

750g beef mince
1 cup breadcrumbs
1 egg, beaten
Dash Tabasco sauce
1xtin of smoked oysters

chicken burgers

Cooking time: around 15 minutes. Makes 4 rissoles

Combine all ingredients in a bowl and mix well. Using wet hands shape into 4 rissoles.

Cook on oiled barbecue plate.

Tip ~ These are delicious served on lightly toasted buns as a burger with salad and satay sauce or mango chutney.

500g chicken mince
½ cup dried breadcrumbs
1 garlic clove, crushed
2 tablespoons lemon juice
1 egg
¼ cup water
Salt and pepper to taste

tuna rissoles

Cooking time: around 15 minutes. Makes 12 rissoles

1x425g tin of tuna
8 potatoes, boiled and mashed
1 onion, finely chopped
1 egg, beaten
Salt and pepper to taste
Plain flour

Combine well drained tuna, mashed potatoes and onion. Add egg and seasonings. Mix well.

Form into 12 rissoles and lightly roll in flour. If possible refrigerate for at least an hour to set.

Cook rissoles on well oiled barbecue plate until golden brown.

Tip ~ Replace the tuna with salmon.

lentil rissoles

Cooking time: around 15 minutes. Makes 6 rissoles

2 cups cooked lentils (red or yellow)
1 egg
½ cup dry biscuit crumbs
1 onion, finely chopped
¼ cup tomato sauce

Combine lentils, egg, biscuit crumbs and onion. Mix well. Add tomato sauce and combine well until mixture is moist and holds together. Make into 6 rissoles. Wet hands make this an easier task.

Fry on well oiled barbecue plate until brown on both sides.

Tip ~ Add a pinch of your favourite spice.

tex mex burgers

Cooking time: around 15 minutes. Makes 4 burgers

500g beef mince
1 small onion, finely chopped
1 small green capsicum, finely chopped
2 tablespoons of salsa or taco sauce
1 crushed garlic clove
oil

Combine mince, onion, capsicum, garlic and salsa/sauce. Season with salt and pepper to taste. Shape into four large burgers and place in fridge for a while.

Cook burgers on lightly oiled barbecue plate.

Serve burgers in warmed tortillas with avocado, tomato, lettuce and extra salsa or taco sauce.

fish

Whether camped beside the ocean or an inland river, fishing is a favourite activity while camping. For a change why not try one of the following recipes.

hints for barbecuing fish

• For best results when barbecuing fish cook over a bed of hot coals – do not cook over open flame.

• Fillets and cutlets should be marinated to add flavour and moisture. Baste while cooking with marinade to stop fish drying out.

• Fillets and cutlets should be placed on a well greased barbecue plate or grill.

• Large whole fish is best wrapped in greased foil, fill cavity of fish with herbs and lemon or orange slices for extra flavour.

beer drinkers trout

Cooking time: around 10-15 minutes. Ingredients per person

Gut, scale and clean trout. Rub inside of trout with butter and fold bacon inside.

Rub outside of trout with butter. Place trout onto foil. Ensure foil is doubled. Splash some beer in and wrap foil around trout, ensuring that parcel is well sealed.

Throw on the barbecue and cook whilst finishing off the beer, cooking time depends on size of trout.

1 trout
1 bacon rasher
Butter
Can/stubbie of beer

chinese style trout

Cooking time: around 10 minutes. Ingredients per person

Combine soy sauce, lemon juice, tomato sauce and good pinch of dried rosemary. Place cleaned and gutted trout in marinade and leave for at least an hour. Turn once.

Place trout into a piece of buttered aluminium foil and wrap trout, ensuring the packet is well sealed. Wrap in second layer of foil

Barbecue over a low fire for about 10 minutes, depending on size of fish, turning once.

Serve trout with remaining marinade.

1 trout
¼ cup soy sauce
1 tablespoon lemon juice
¼ cup tomato sauce
dried rosemary

lemon and garlic fish

Cooking time: around 10-15 minutes. Serves 4

1-2 firm white fish fillets,
per person
MARINADE
1 teaspoon lemon rind,
grated
½ cup lemon juice
2 tablespoons oil
2 garlic cloves, crushed
2 tablespoons white wine
1 teaspoon sugar
½ teaspoon pepper

Combine all marinade ingredients in a shallow dish. Add fish cutlets and coat with mixture. Leave to marinate for a couple of hours.

Cook fish cutlets on lightly greased hot barbecue plate until tender.

honeyed fish fillets

Cooking time: around 10-15 minutes. Serves 4

4 large firm white fish fillets
MARINADE
3 tablespoons honey
1 teaspoon soy sauce
¼ teaspoon chilli powder
1 teaspoon ginger powder
1 tablespoon orange juice
1 onion, finely chopped
Pepper taste

Mix marinade ingredients and gently heat to melt honey. Score fish fillets and place in deep dish. Pour marinade over fish and leave for a few hours.

Oil barbecue plate and cook fish on each side, around 3 minutes, until cooked. Baste with marinade during cooking.

fruity stuffed whole bream

Cooking time: depends on fish size. Serves 2

2 medium whole bream
½ cup dried fruit medley
½ cup breadcrumbs
½ cup cooked rice
½ cup grated tasty cheese
2 tablespoons lemon juice
1 egg

Combine dried fruit, breadcrumbs, rice, cheese, juice and egg. Mix well.

Spoon mixture into fish and dot with butter.

Wrap fish firmly in double layer of aluminium foil.

Barbecue on plate or on grill until fish is tender.

bullockies bbq loaf

This is a great way of bringing some life and flavour back to day old bread or rolls.

Combine butter with seasonings until well mixed.

Slice bread nearly all the way through at 2cm intervals. Spread each side of the bread with butter.

Wrap in foil and cook over hot coals on grill or barbecue plate for 15-20 minutes until heated through, turning around for all sides to be cooked.

1 tank loaf or similar, eg: Vienna, French stick or bread rolls

BUTTER 1

1 cup butter

2 teaspoons dried mixed herbs

2 cloves garlic, crushed

BUTTER 2

1 cup butter

Hand full of finely chopped meat, spicy meats are great ie: pastrami or salami

¼ cup grated cheese, parmesan gives good taste

1 tablespoon dried mixed herbs

BUTTER 3

1 cup butter

1 tablespoon curry powder

2 teaspoons Worcestershire sauce

Barbecues are an essential piece of bush cooking equipment.

FRYING PAN COOKING

A frying pan of some description is a valuable asset to your bush cooking equipment. Try out a few of these recipes in the frying pan and you'll never leave home without one again.

hawkers mince

Cooking time: 20-25 minutes. Serves 4

Heat oil in frying pan. Cook onion and capsicum until tender.

Add mince and brown. Add mustard powder, cayenne pepper and salt and pepper to taste. Mix well.

Carefully stir in potatoes and heat through, approximately 10 minutes.

Tip ~ This is a quick and easy meal to prepare, the mustard powder and cayenne pepper adding a bite to the mince. You can serve this with your favourite sauce for additional flavour.

750g beef mince
1 onion, chopped
1 capsicum, chopped
1 garlic clove, crushed
¾ teaspoon mustard powder
¼ teaspoon cayenne pepper
2-3 potatoes cubed, boiled but slightly firm

simple spaghetti bolognaise

Cooking time: 20-25 minutes. Serves 4

Gently fry onion, capsicum and garlic in oil in large frying pan. Add mince and brown.

Add crushed tomatoes, tomato paste and beef stock cube. Add a dash of Worcestershire sauce, olives and sprinkle of herbs.

Bring to the boil then simmer over low heat for 10-15 minutes until sauce has thickened.

Serve over pasta of choice with parmesan cheese.

Tip ~ Additional vegetables such as mushrooms can be added. If you prefer a sauce with more moisture add some red wine or water and reduce simmer time.

500g beef mince
Crushed garlic to taste
1 onion, chopped
1 capsicum, chopped
1x420g crushed tomatoes
1x140g tub tomato paste
Beef stock cube
Dash Worcestershire sauce
Sliced black olives
Dried Italian herbs, to taste

middle eastern lamb

Cooking time: 15 minutes. Serves 4-6

Heat some oil in frying pan. Fry onion until lighly browned. Add mince and cook over high heat until well browned and any liquid has evaporated.

Add eggplant and next four ingredients. Bring to boil then move to low heat and simmer covered for 10 minutes or until eggplant is tender. Stir in pinenuts if using.

Tip ~ This mince is great served in pita pockets or lavash wraps with lettuce, carrot, beetroot and some plain yoghurt.

500g lamb mince
1 onion, chopped
1 eggplant, cut into 1cm cubes
2 teaspoons garam masala
1/2 cup chicken stock
1/2 cup tomato puree
1/3 cup sultanas
2 tablespoons pinenuts, optional

Both Craig and I love Mexican food, so we have included a few of our favourite recipes that can be enjoyed in the bush just as much as at home.

outback chilli

Cooking time: 30 minutes. Serves 4

500g beef mince
1 onion, finely chopped
1 capsicum, finely chopped
1-2 cloves of garlic, crushed
1x420g tin of tomato soup
1x440g tin red kidney beans, drained
1 beef stock cube
Chilli powder to taste

Fry onion, capsicum and garlic in a little oil in frying pan. Add mince and brown.

Add tomato soup, drained red kidney beans, stock cube and chilli powder. Stir to combine all ingredients and simmer for approximately 20 minutes.

Delicious served with boiled rice and sour cream.

Tip ~ To ensure there isn't too much heat when adding chilli, add in small amounts mix through and leave for a minute before tasting. Add extra if necessary.

bush-style mexican fajitas

We've included this recipe, not only because it is one of our favourites, but also as it's easy to make and a nice change from barbecues and the like. Besides, it's always a favourite with the kids.

Cooking time: 15-20 minutes. Serves 4-6

500g chicken strips
1 large onion, sliced
1 capsicum, sliced
Packet of Old El Paso Fajita Rub mix
¼ cup water
Packet tortillas
Taco sauce

TO SERVE
shredded lettuce, grated cheese, tomato slices, taco sauce and sour cream

Combine Fajita Rub mix with water. Set aside.

Heat oil in frying pan. Add onion and capsicum, cook until tender, remove from pan.

Add to pan chicken strips and fry until just cooked. Return vegetables to pan along with sauce mix and heat through until chicken and vegetables are well covered with sauce, add extra water if necessary.

Meanwhile heat tortillas in foil over coals.

Now here comes the fun part. Serve the chicken mixture on the heated tortillas with taco sauce, lettuce, cheese and tomato. Fold tortilla and serve with sour cream.

Tip ~ This recipe makes enough for 9-12 tortillas depending on how hungry you are. For something different you could use either beef or if you're near the seaside, prawns, instead of the chicken.

south of the border beef stir fry

Cooking time: 15-20 minutes. Serves 4

Combine beef strips and taco seasoning. Heat oil in frying pan and cook beef and onion in batches until beef is browned. Remove from frying pan.

Stir fry capsicums until tender. Return beef and onion to pan with tomato and 2 tablespoons of chopped coriander leaves, if you have. Cook until heated through.

Serve with boiled rice.

Tip ~ The fresh coriander is great in this dish, so if you can get it do so. Then, so as not to waste it, do as we do and cook all the meals with fresh coriander over the next couple of days such as the cous cous salad, thai salad and the home made salsa. However if you don't have or can't get fresh, use minced coriander that comes in a tube or jar.

750g beef strips
1 packet taco seasoning
1 red onion, sliced
2 capsicums, sliced
4 tomatoes sliced
Coriander leaves, optional

mexican quesadillas

Cooking time: 5-10 minutes. Serves 2

Use a frying pan to fit the tortillas. These are cooked dry, do not oil or grease the frying pan.

Heat a dry frying pan. Place one tortilla in pan and spread with taco sauce. Cook for about 2 minutes

Then place shredded chicken, spring onions and grated cheese over sauce, and place second tortilla on top. Cook for another 2 minutes.

Heres the tricky bit - place a plate over pan and tip out tortilla. Then slide tortilla back into pan and cook second side until heated through and cheese has melted.

Cut into wedges and serve with sour cream and a sprinkle of paprika.

Tip ~ Any type of cooked meat can be used in this dish.

2 flour tortillas
Taco sauce
Barbecue chicken, meat shredded
2 spring onions, finely chopped
Grated cheese
Sour cream
Paprika

choice chicken curry

Cooking time: 30-40 minutes. Serves 4

1kg chicken thighs, diced	Season flour with black pepper. Coat diced chicken with seasoned flour, shake off excess.
Seasoned flour	
1-2 tablespoons curry powder, or to taste	Brown chicken pieces in oil in large frying pan, remove and drain.
2 onions, sliced	Add onions and garlic to frying pan and cook until soft. Add curry powder and stir until fragrant.
2 garlic cloves, crushed	
1x440g tin crushed tomatoes	Return chicken to frying pan with tomatoes, chicken stock cube and water. Bring to the boil, move to lower heat and simmer until chicken is tender.
1 chicken stock cube	Stir regularly to stop sticking, if necessary add extra water.
½ cup water	Serve with boiled rice.

chicken jambalaya

Cooking time: 40 minutes. Serves 4

Oil	Heat oil in a large frying pan. Add onion and cook until soft, about 5 minutes.
1½ cups cooked chicken	
1 onion, finely chopped	Add rice and vegetables and stir until well combined. Add tomato puree, water, basil and Worcestershire sauce. Mix well and bring to boil.
1 cup rice	
1 cup vegetables of choice	
1 cup tomato puree	Move to lower heat and simmer covered until rice and vegetables are tender and liquid is absorbed, approximately 30 minutes.
1 cup water	
½ teaspoon dried basil	Add chicken and season with salt and pepper. Stir well until heated through.
1 tablespoon Worcestershire sauce	
	Tip ~ This is a great recipe to use up left over roast or barbecue chicken, otherwise stir fry 2 to 3 diced chicken breasts. For a different flavour add some ham or some spicy sausage.

sweet & sour chicken stir-fry

Serves 4

750g chicken strips	Coat chicken strips with cornflour, shake off excess. Heat oil in frying pan and quickly stir-fry meat until well browned, remove from pan.
1 tablespoon cornflour	
1x305g tin sweet & sour sauce	Heat extra oil in pan and add vegetables and stir-fry until tender. Return meat to pan with sweet and sour sauce, stir well and heat through.
1 onion, cut in wedges	
1 capsicum, sliced	Serve with boiled or fried rice.
1 carrot, sliced	Tip ~ Chicken can be replaced with pork or firm fish fillets. Other vegetables that can be added are shallots, celery or even some cucumber with the seeds scooped out.
1 garlic clove, crushed, optional	

quick and easy tuna mornay

Cooking time: 10-15 minutes. Serves 2-3

Melt butter in frying pan, add onion and capsicum and fry for 3 minutes. Add flour and stir constantly until well mixed.

Slowly add milk and cream stirring until mixture thickens. Stir in cheese, corn, tuna, a good dash of Worcestershire sauce and salt and pepper to taste.

Mix well until heated through. Serve with pasta.

Tip ~ For a sweeter mornay add a small tin of drained crushed pineapple. Alternatively, the mornay can be mixed through the pasta and poured into a tin with additional cheese on top and baked in the camp oven with coals on top until the cheese melts and browns.

2 tablespoons butter
1 large onion, chopped
½ capsicum, chopped
1 tablespoon flour
¾ cup milk
½ cup cream
⅓ cup grated cheese
1x310g can corn kernels, drained
1x185g can tuna, drained
Worcestershire sauce
Salt and pepper to taste

tuna curry

Cooking time: 15 minutes. Serves 4

Heat oil in frying pan, add onion and capsicum, cook until soft. Add flour and curry powder, stir in well and cook for 1 minute.

Combine water, milk and stock cube. Gradually add to pan, stirring until mixture boils and thickens slightly.

Move to lower heat and simmer for 10 minutes. Add tuna, cream and lemon juice. Stir until well mixed and heated through.

Oil
1 onion, sliced
1 capsicum, sliced
⅓ cup plain flour
1 tablespoon curry powder, or more to taste
¾ cup milk
3 cups water
1 chicken stock cube
1x425g can tuna, drained
¼ cup cream
Juice of 1 lemon

easy macaroni & cheese

Cooking time: 30 minutes. Serves 4

1 cup macaroni pasta, cooked

1 tablespoon butter

2 tablespoons plain flour

2 teaspoons dry mustard

1 ½ cups milk

¾ cup grated tasty cheese

1 teaspoon dried mixed herbs

Melt butter in frying pan. Add flour and mustard and stir until mixture bubbles.

Remove from heat and gradually stir in milk until well mixed.

Return pan to heat and stir until mixture boils and thickens. Add cheese and stir until melted. Add macaroni and herbs and gently stir until well mixed.

Tip ~ Drained tuna, salmon or vegetables can be added to this dish.

dinkum curried snags

Cooking time: 15-20 minutes. Serves 4

2-3 sausages per person

2 onions, chopped

1 large apple, peeled and chopped

2 teaspoons curry powder or to taste

Sultanas

2 beef stock cubes

2 cups water

2 teaspoons corn flour

Cook sausages in frying pan until just cooked. Remove and drain.

In frying pan cook onion and apple in a little oil until onions are soft. Add curry powder to frying pan and stir. Add beef stock cube and water and bring to the boil. Combine corn flour with a small amount of liquid from the pan and add to the pan. Put frying pan over moderate coals to let sauce simmer. Add sausages, either whole or sliced, and a handful of sultanas.

Simmer until heated through and sauce has thickened.

Serve with boiled rice or mashed potato.

Tip ~ For a different taste, add some chopped bacon with the onion.

creamy bacon & mushroom sauce

Cooking time: approximately 20 minutes. Serves 4

4 rashers of bacon, chopped

1 onion, chopped

2 cups of mushrooms, sliced

Crushed garlic to taste

1x300ml carton cream

1 tablespoon grated parmesan cheese

Good dash Worcestershire sauce

Black pepper

Fry bacon, onion and garlic in a little oil until tender. Add mushrooms and heat through.

Place pan over moderate coals and add cream, parmesan cheese, Worcestershire sauce and pepper to taste.

Cook over low heat stirring until sauce thickens – do not let boil.

Serve over pasta of choice.

Tip ~ Evaporated milk can replace the cream for a lighter sauce.

spicy tomato and bacon sauce for pasta

Cooking time: 20 minutes. Serves 4

Fry bacon, onion and garlic in hot oil in frying pan. Add crushed tomatoes, tomato paste, chilli powder, Tabasco sauce to taste, a good sprinkle of Italian herbs and olives if using.

Move to lower heat and simmer for 15 minutes until sauce thickens.

Serve over pasta of choice with parmesan cheese.

6 bacon rashers, rind removed and diced

1 onion, chopped

1 garlic clove, crushed

1x420g tinned crushed tomatoes

1x140g tin tomato paste

Chilli powder to taste

Tabasco sauce

Italian herbs

1 tablespoon sliced black olives, optional

cath's best fried rice

Cooking time: 15-20 minutes. Serves 4

Cook rice the night before or at breakfast and keep in fridge or esky until ready to use.

Heat oil in frying pan and cook bacon and shallots in a little oil with garlic until tender. Remove from pan and drain on paper towel.

Put a little more oil in frying pan and add beaten eggs. Do not stir, move pan around for egg to cook in a thin layer. Cook egg until firm, then slice into strips with knife or egg flip. Remove from pan and drain on paper towel with bacon mixture.

Add a little more oil to frying pan and add rice. Heat through. Add bacon, shallots and egg. Mix thoroughly.

Season with lemon pepper and soy sauce to taste.

Tip ~ To get the best results for fried rice the rice needs to be really dry and well separated. The best way of doing this is to drain the rice well after cooking and spread out on a tray or plates lined with paper towel then left in the fridge or ice box. When we cook fried rice in the bush we cook the rice the night before as soon as we set up camp, drain it well then spread it out on plates on paper towel to dry whilst we are still up. Then when we go to bed we transfer the rice to a bowl or container lined with paper towel and leave in the fridge till the next night.

Oil

1-2 cups of cold boiled rice

2 bacon rashers, diced

1 garlic clove, crushed

4 shallots, thinly sliced

2 eggs, beaten

Lemon pepper seasoning

Soy sauce

For those who might be lucky enough to catch some yabbies or marron whilst out camping, here's a few hints and recipes.

How to kill a yabby? There are a few different methods: a) Place the fresh yabby into the freezer to slow down its metabolism until it dies; b) stab the yabby with a sharp knife in the centre of the head just behind the eyes - this is ideal if you wish to BBQ the yabby; c) possibly the most popular way, and more practical if camping when you don't have a freezer, bring a very large pot of water to a rapid boil, plunge the yabby into the boiling water and boil until the yabby turns red. Make sure you don't overcrowd the pot.

col watson's chilli yabbies

Cooking time: 10 minutes. Serves 4

1 kg cooked yabby tails
1 garlic clove, crushed
2 teaspoons minced ginger
1 onion, chopped
2 tomatoes cut into wedges
1 teaspoon Tabasco sauce
2 tablespoons tomato sauce
1 tablespoon soy sauce
½ cup water

Fry garlic, ginger and onion in oil until fragrant.

Add tomato wedges, sauces and water, bring to the boil. Boil for 2 minutes.

Add cooked yabbies and heat through.

Serve with boiled or steamed rice.

yabbies in wine

Cooking time: 10 minutes. Serves 4

1 kg cooked yabby tails
1 onion, diced
1 garlic clove, crushed
½ cup white wine
1 cup cream
Ground black pepper

Heat oil in frying pan. Fry onion and garlic until transparent.

Add wine and cream and simmer for a 2 minutes.

Add yabbies and heat through. Season with ground black pepper.

Serve with boiled or steamed rice.

OPPOSITE: Col Watson — The Yabby King — with a good sized yabby ready for the pot.

CAMP OVEN COOKING

Without doubt a camp oven is the quintessential piece of bush cooking equipment. Once you've mastered the art of cooking in a camp oven these recipes will become standard fare on your camping adventures.

using your camp oven

• You will get the best results from your camp oven cooking if you follow a few simple tried and tested procedures.

• Place the oven on or over the main fire to get it nice and hot before you place any food inside. A tripod or grate is ideal for this task. By doing this you wont be drawing heat from the coals to heat the oven.

• If you are cooking recipes that require most of the heat to be coming from the top, then make sure that you get the lid of the oven hot also.

• If you are baking or roasting, when the oven is hot place it on a thin bed of coals a little way from the main fire and put in your food to be cooked. Now place coals on the lid.

• For recipes that require browning heap coals in the centre of the lid to produce a more concentrated heat.

• Bedourie ovens tend to cook better if they are placed in a shallow hole with coals on the bottom and half buried up the sides with hot ash and embers, and some coals on the lid.

• When baking place a trivet or cake rack inside your camp oven. This allows the heat to circulate better and helps avoid burning your food on the base of the oven.

• The type of wood you are burning for coals will dictate how often you need to replenish coals under and on the lid of the camp oven.

Always have a good supply of coals on hand when cooking in your camp oven.

• Try to minimise how often you remove the lid from your oven. Check on dampers and breads after 20 minutes and roasts after 30-40 minutes. Excessive lifting of the lid allows heat to escape and results in longer cooking times.

• When cleaning your cast iron camp oven never pour cold water into a hot oven as it may cause the oven to crack. *Always* use warm or hot water.

• Take care not to drop cast iron camp ovens on hard surfaces such as rocks or concrete. Cast iron is brittle and you could easily crack your oven.

camp oven temperatures

To assess the temperature in a camp oven place a piece of newspaper or paper towel inside the oven for approximately 5 minutes. Rule of thumb is:

If paper is black and smoking – *the oven is too hot.*

If paper is a light brown to yellow colour – *the oven is moderate to hot.*

If paper is a cream or pale yellow colour – *the oven is slow to moderate.*

When cooking on wet or damp ground you need to allow extra cooking time.

roasting in a camp oven

Cooking a roast in the bush in a camp oven is really no different to cooking one at home. The main difference is you need to check the heat of the coals regularly to ensure your meat is cooking evenly. The best way of doing this is to have plenty of hot coals ready, so each time you check the meat, say every 30-40 minutes, you have some new coals to place on the lid and shovel around the camp oven.

Cooking times for roasts depends on the size of the meat and heat of your coals, that's why it's important to check the meat regularly!

1. Ensure camp oven is well oiled. Place oven over fire to get it nice and hot.

2. Place meat in camp oven and cover with lid.

3. Place camp oven in hot coals and shovel coals on lid.

4. Depending on the size of the meat, cook for one to two and a half hours.

5. Vegetables cut into serving sizes, eg: potato, pumpkin, sweet potato or onion can be added in the last 40-45 minutes.

6. Before carving, let the meat stand for at least 5-10 minutes for juices to flow out, keep it warm by covering with aluminium foil.

7. Serve meat with vegetables and gravy/sauce of choice. There is now a large range of instant gravies available that are easy to carry and make by simply adding boiling water to the gravy mix.

roast lamb seasonings

A. Rub dried rosemary over the lamb.

B. Rub a mixture of crushed garlic and dried rosemary over the lamb.

C. Cut slits in the lamb and place whole garlic cloves in.

D. A herbed mustard made from: 3 tablespoons French mustard, 3 teaspoons soy sauce, 1 clove of garlic, 1 teaspoon rosemary and oil mixed to a smooth paste can be rubbed/ brushed over the leg.

roast beef seasonings

A. Rub a mixture of seeded mustard and red wine over beef.

B. Make a spicy rub from: 1 teaspoon ground cumin, $\frac{1}{2}$ teaspoon chilli powder, 2 crushed garlic cloves and $\frac{1}{2}$ teaspoon salt. Combine together and rub into beef, and drizzle some oil over.

roast chicken

1. Remove the neck and any giblets in the cavity, rinse thoroughly and dry with paper towel.

2. Brush melted butter over bird.

3. Roast chicken breast side up for 15 minutes in camp oven over flame.

4. Turn chicken over and place camp oven on coals and cook for 50-60 minutes.

Chicken is cooked when juices run clear from thigh when pierced with a skewer and when a leg rocks easily in the socket.

roast chicken seasonings

A. Rub dried mixed herbs, salt and pepper over bird after brushing with butter.

B. Place $\frac{1}{2}$ lemon in cavity with dried oregano or marjoram.

C. Place knob of butter, crushed garlic cloves and dried rosemary in cavity.

D. Combine $1\frac{1}{2}$ cups of breadcrumbs, one finely chopped celery stick, one finely chopped onion, 1 teaspoon of dried mixed herbs and 1 lightly beaten egg. Fill chicken cavity, do not pack too tightly.

beef casserole with dumplings

Cooking time: 2 hours. Serves 4-6

Lightly toss meat in seasoned flour, shake off excess. Heat oil in camp oven and brown meat. Add onions and cook until brown.

Combine beef stock, Worcestershire sauce and soy sauce and pour over beef and onions. Cover and cook on medium coals for 1 hour to 1¼ hours.

Add capsicum and carrots, bake for further 20-30 minutes until meat is tender.

Place dumplings (see recipe below) on top of casserole. Brush dumplings with extra milk.

Replace camp oven lid and place coals on top and bake for 15 minutes until dumplings are golden and puffed.

Tip ~ We regularly cook this favourite dish at home in our wood stove during the winter months. It cooks just as good in the bush in a camp oven.

1kg chuck steak, cubed
Oil
½ cup seasoned flour
2 medium onions, diced
1 capsicum, diced
2 small carrots, diced
1½ cups beef stock
2 tablespoons Worcestershire sauce
1 tablespoon soy sauce

doughboy's dumplings

Place flour in bowl. Rub butter into flour using fingers to make a fine crumbly texture.

Add milk, cheese and herbs. Mix thoroughly.

Place onto floured surface and knead until smooth. Pull apart into rough balls and place dumplings on top of casserole, brush with milk.

1 cup self-raising flour
2 tablespoons butter
2-3 tablespoons milk
⅓ cup grated cheddar cheese
1 teaspoon of dried mix herbs - optional

south coast stew

Cooking time: 40 minutes. Serves 4-6

Heat oil in camp oven and stir in flour. Cook, stirring frequently, until flour turns a dark brown and mixture has thickened.

Add celery, onion and capsicum. Cook until tender. Add curry powder and cook for 1 minute.

Add tomotoes and their liquid, water, sugar and salt. Bring to boil.

Move to low heat and add fish chunks. Bake over low heat for 20-30 minutes, until fish flakes easily with a fork.

Tip ~ Half the fish and add 500g of uncooked prawns to this dish.

1kg thick fish fillets, cut into chunks
¼ cup oil
¼ cup plain flour
2 celery sticks, diced
1 onion, diced
1 capsicum, diced
1 tablespoon curry powder
1x800g tin tomatoes
¼ cup water
2 teaspoon sugar
Salt to taste

teamsters beef & beans

Cooking time: Approximately 1½ hours. Serves 4

500g chuck steak, cubed	Brown beef in camp oven in hot oil. Add onion and cook until soft.
1 onion, chopped	
2 tablespoons paprika	Sprinkle paprika over beef and onions. Combine water and stock cubes. Pour over meat and mix well. Cover and cook until meat is tender – 1-1½ hours, adding water if needed.
2 beef stock cubes	
¾ cup warm water	
1x420g can baked beans	When meat is tender add baked beans and cook for further 10-15 minutes.
	Delicious served with potatoes and bread.

travellers stew

Cooking time: 1 hour 45 minutes to 2 hours. Serves 4-6

750g chuck steak, cubed	Toss meat in flour, shake off excess.
¼ cup flour	Heat oil in camp oven and brown meat. Remove and drain on paper towels.
Oil	
2 onions, sliced	Place sliced potatoes in bottom of camp oven. Place meat, onions and carrots on top of potatoes. Add some black pepper.
2 large potatoes, peeled and thickly sliced	
2 carrots, sliced thickly	Pour in beer, beef stock and soy sauce. Throw in bay leaves if using. Bake in camp oven uncovered on a grill above medium coals until meat is tender, around 1½ to 2 hours.
1 can beer	
1 cup beef stock	
1 tablespoon soy sauce	Serve with freshly made damper or fresh bread.
2 bay leaves, if you have them	

beef hot pot

Cooking time: 1 hour 30 minutes. Serves 4

750g blade steak, cubed	Heat oil in camp oven over hot coals and brown meat.
Oil	Combine Hot Pot Base, water and tomatoes and pour over meat.
1 packet Curry Hot Pot Casserole Base	
1½ cups water	Cook covered in camp oven until meat is tender, approximately 1½ hours.
1x410g tinned tomatoes	

cooee stew

Cooking time: 1 hour 10 minutes. Serves 6

Brown chicken on all sides in hot oil in camp oven. Remove and drain on paper towel.

Cook onion in camp oven until soft. Add potatoes and capsicum. Stir well to mix with onions.

Return chicken to camp oven with tomatoes, stock, cayenne pepper and Worcestershire sauce. Bring to the boil, season with salt.

Move to medium heat and simmer for 45 to 50 minutes. Add corn and cook for a further 15 minutes until chicken is tender.

Mix flour and butter together. Add to the pan gradually, stirring as you go. Adjust seasonings if necessary and cook for further 5 minutes.

2kg chicken pieces
1 large onion, sliced
2 large potatoes, peeled and cut into 2cm cubes
1 green capsicum, chopped
3 tomatoes, quartered
1 ½ cups chicken stock
¼ teaspoon cayenne pepper
1 ½ tablespoons Worcestershire sauce
1x420g tin sweetcorn kernels, drained
1 tablespoon plain flour
1 tablespoon butter

black stump casserole

Cooking time: Approximately 2 hours 45 minutes. Serves 4-6

Coat meat with flour and shake off excess.

Heat oil in camp oven and brown meat. Add onions and cook until golden. Add extra oil or butter if necessary.

Add garlic, sugar, vinegar, herbs and salt and pepper to taste. Pour in beer and mix well.

Cover and cook over medium coals for 2-2 ½ hours until meat is tender and gravy thick, stirring occasionally.

Tip ~ This casserole is delicious served with potatoes, either mashed or just boiled, or even by itself with some fresh bread to mop up the gravy.

2kg chuck steak, cubed
4 tablespoons plain flour
4 large onions, sliced
1 can of beer, not cold
2 cloves garlic, crushed
4 teaspoons of brown sugar
2 tablespoons vinegar
1 bay leaf
1 teaspoon dried mixed herbs
Salt and pepper to taste

diggers meat loaf

Cooking time: 1 hour. Serves 6-8

500g beef mince
1 large onion, chopped
2 cloves garlic, crushed
1x140g tub tomato paste
2 tablespoon Worcestershire sauce
1 carrot, grated
1 cup corn kernels
½ cup peas
1 teaspoon mixed herbs
1 egg, beaten
1 ½ cup breadcrumbs

Combine all ingredients and place into greased loaf tin. If you don't have a loaf tin you can shape this into a loaf and wrap well in foil.

Cook in camp oven over medium coals for 1 hour or until cooked through. Drain off excess juices before cutting.

Tip ~ For a change, use different vegetables. Left overs of this meat loaf are great in sandwiches the next day. Other variations on this basic meat loaf is to line the loaf tin with bacon slices; place a couple of hard boiled eggs down the centre of the loaf prior to cooking; or cover the cooked meat loaf with mashed potato then brush with melted butter and return to camp oven for a further 15 minutes with coals on the lid and cook until browned.

dee's chow mein

Cooking time: 30-40 minutes. Serves 4

500g mince
1 onion, finely chopped
1 carrot, grated
¼ cabbage, shredded
Handful of rice
1 packet of 2 minute chicken noodles, crushed
Curry powder to taste
Water

Heat oil in camp oven and fry onion until tender. Add mince and brown.

Add carrot, cabbage, crushed noodles and rice adding enough water to cover all ingredients. Add the flavour sachet from noodles and curry powder to taste.

Allow to simmer until rice and noodles are cooked through. Adding extra water if necessary.

Serve with crusty fresh bread or damper and sauce of your choice.

Tip ~ Left overs are tasty cold on sandwiches with tomato sauce.

moroccan lamb

Cooking time: 1 hour 10 minutes. Serves 4

Heat oil in camp oven over hot coals. Cook lamb in hot oil until well browned.

Add stock, onion, fruit and seasonings to camp oven. Simmer covered until meat is tender approximately 1 hour.

Serve with either boiled rice or couscous and fresh bread.

750g lamb, cubed
Oil
2 cups chicken stock
2 onions, finely chopped
½ cup pitted prunes, halved
½ cup dried apricots, halved
1 teaspoon powdered ginger
1 teaspoon ground cinnamon

flame'n good curry

Cooking time: 1 hour 15 minutes. Serves 4–6

Heat oil and brown meat in camp oven. Add onion, garlic and ginger to pan and cook until onion is tender.

Stir in chilli powder, cardamon and turmeric and cook until fragrant. Add beef stock and cook covered over medium coals until meat is nearly tender, depending on coals around 30-45 minutes.

Add potatoes and cook uncovered until meat and potatoes are tender.

Serve with rice.

750g round steak, cubed
Oil
3 onions, chopped
4 garlic cloves, crushed
1 tablespoon crushed ginger
1 teaspoon chilli powder
2 teaspoons ground cardamon
2 teaspoons turmeric
1½ cups beef stock
6 potatoes, peeled and cubed

jumbuck stew

Cooking time: 1 hour 30 minutes. Serves 4-6

*8 medium potatoes, peeled
and thickly sliced
1kg lamb chops
4 large onions, thickly sliced
2 cups chicken stock
2 bay leaves
Ground pepper*

Trim chops of any excess fat.

Arrange half the potato slices in the bottom of heated camp oven, or in a dish to fit in the camp oven. Place meat and onions on top of potatoes, then arrange the balance of potato slices on top.

Pour in chicken stock, add bay leaves and ground pepper to taste.

Cover and cook with medium heat coals around the camp oven and on the lid for 1½ hours until the chops are tender.

Tip ~ To ensure potatoes do not stick to the base of the camp oven, do not put coals directly under the camp oven. The potatoes will break down during cooking and thickens the stock.

italian lamb casserole

Cooking time: 1 hour 30 minutes. Serves 4-6

*1.5kg diced lamb
½ cup plain flour
4 celery sticks, sliced
2 medium carrots, sliced
2 large onions, sliced
2 cloves crushed garlic
1x410g tinned tomatoes
¼ cup tomato paste
1 cup white wine
1 cup chicken stock
¾ teaspoon dried oregano
¾ teaspoon dried thyme
½ teaspoon dried rosemary*

Toss lamb in flour and shake off excess. Brown meat in oil in hot camp oven in batches until browned, drain on paper towels.

Add balance of ingredients and bring to the boil.

Return lamb to camp oven, season with slat and pepper. Cover and bake in medium coals for 1 hour, or until lamb is tender.

Tip ~ This tasty casserole can be served with mash and vegetables, or even with pasta. Don't forget some fresh bread or damper!

baked chops with tomatoes

Cooking time: 1 hour. Serves 4–6

Place chops in deep dish. Mix oil, wine, thyme, salt and pepper together and then pour over chops. Cover and marinate in fridge for 1 hour.

Combine crushed tomatoes, capsicum, onion and garlic.

Place lamb chops in warmed camp oven, or in dish in camp oven, and spoon tomato topping over.

Cook in camp oven in medium to hot coals for 1 hour until chops are cooked through.

Serve with mash potato or rice.

4-6 large lamb chops of choice
2 tablespoons oil
3 tablespoons red wine
1 tablespoon dried thyme
Salt and pepper
TOMATO TOPPING
1X410g tin crushed tomatoes
1 capsicum, diced
1 red onion, diced
2 crushed garlic cloves

lamb & mushie stew

Cooking time: 2 hours. Serves 4

Trim lamb chops of any excess fat. Heat some oil in camp oven and brown chops, drain on paper towels. Once all chops are browned return to camp oven.

Mix together the soup, sauce, stock and wine. Pour over chops.

Bake in camp oven in medium coals for 1½ hours.

Cook mushrooms in a frying pan in a little oil until brown, then stir through the stew. Cook for a further ½ hour or until the meat is tender.

4-6 large lamb leg chops
1x440g tin cream of mushroom soup
¼ cup chicken stock
½ cup red wine
250g button mushrooms, sliced

hargraves reward

Cooking time: about 1 hour. Serves 4-6

500g topside steak, cubed
Oil
3 large carrots, sliced
1 large onion cut into rings
2 tablespoons of Gravox Powder
2 cups water
½ cup of plain flour
Salt and pepper to taste

Heat oil in camp oven over hot coals.

Toss steak in flour seasoned with salt and pepper. Cook steak in hot oil until browned. Remove steak and drain excess oil.

Add sliced carrot and onion to camp oven and place steak on top. Mix Gravox and water and pour over meat and vegetables.

Cook slowly in camp oven until meat is tender, approximately 1 hour.

Serve with either boiled or mashed potato and fresh damper.

outback osso bucco

Cooking time: 2 hours. Serves 6

1 to 2 osso bucco pieces per person
2 cups plain flour, seasoned
Oil
1 large onion, diced
2 garlic cloves crushed
1 large carrot, sliced
⅔ cup white wine
⅔ cup beef stock
1x410g tin tomatoes, crushed
¼ cup tomato paste
½ teaspoon sugar

Heat camp oven over hot coals. Coat osso bucco pieces in seasoned flour, shake off excess.

Heat oil in camp oven and brown meat, drain on paper towels.

Add onion, garlic and carrot to camp oven, cook until onion is soft. Then add wine, stock, undrained tomatoes, tomato paste and sugar. Bring to boil then simmer for 5 minutes.

Return meat to camp oven, cover and bake in low to medium coals until meat is tender, around 1 hour and 45 minutes.

Tip ~ The slow cooking of this dish makes the meat so tender it just falls off the bone. Outback osso bucco tastes even better reheated the next day!

drumsticks in special sauce

Cooking time: 40-60 minutes

Chicken drumsticks, 3-4 per person
Tomato sauce
Worcestershire sauce
Garlic - optional

Place drumsticks in camp oven.

Mix 3 parts tomato sauce to 1 part Worcestershire sauce add garlic if using and slosh sauce over the chicken.

Cook in camp oven over medium coals until tender.

apricot chicken

Cooking time: 40-60 minutes. Serves 4

Toss chicken in seasoned flour, shake off excess.

Heat oil in camp oven and quickly cook chicken until browned. Add onion to camp oven and cook until soft.

Combine French Onion Soup Mix with apricot nectar, pour over chicken. Cover and bake in medium coals on bottom and top until chicken is cooked, about 40 minutes depending on heat of coals stirring occasionally ensuring that chicken is not sticking to bottom.

Stir in apricot halves. Cook uncovered for further 10 minutes until heated through.

Serve with rice or potatoes and vegetables if you have.

8 chicken pieces
¼ cup seasoned flour
1 tablespoon oil
1 onion, sliced
1 packet of French Onion Soup Mix
1x425ml can apricot nectar
1x425g can apricot halves, drained

crunchy chicken bake

Cooking time: 20-30 minutes. Serves 4

Remove chicken from bones and chop. Place in bowl.

Add remaining ingredients except cheese and potato chips. Pour into a lightly greased pie dish. Sprinkle cheese on top then sprinkle potato chips on top of the cheese.

Bake in camp oven with medium coals on base and hot coals on lid for 20 minutes until top is golden brown and heated through.

Tip ~ This is a great meal for your first night at camp as it's easy to prepare and doesn't take too long to cook once you've got the hot coals. Just remember to grab a BBQ chook from the local deli or take away as you're leaving home!

1 barbecue chicken
3 sticks celery, sliced
1 ½ cups mayonnaise
½ cup cream
1 onion, chopped
1 tablespoon lemon juice
1 cup grated tasty cheese
2x25g packets potato chips

sundowner's chicken casserole

Cooking time: 1 hour 30 minutes to 2 hours. Serves 4

8 chicken drumsticks
1 onion, sliced
1 garlic clove, crushed
1 carrot, sliced
1 capsicum, sliced
1 chicken stock cube
¾ cup water
¼ cup red or white wine
1x410g tin of crushed tomatoes
1 teaspoon mixed herbs
Salt and pepper

Fry onion, garlic, carrot and capsicum in hot oil for 3-4 minutes in camp oven. Add chicken and brown.

Add stock cube, water, wine, tomatoes and herbs. Season with salt and pepper.

Cover camp oven and simmer over medium coals for 1½ to 2 hours until chicken is cooked and tender.

Serve over pasta or with boiled rice.

chicken paella

Cooking time: 30 minutes. Serves 4

¼ cup plain flour, seasoned with black pepper
2 chicken breasts, cubed
Oil
2 garlic cloves, crushed
1 capsicum, chopped
1 onion, finely chopped
1 zucchini, sliced
1 cup rice
1x410g tinned tomatoes, chopped
2 cups chicken stock
½ cup peas

Cover chicken in seasoned flour, shake off excess.

Cook chicken in oil in camp oven until browned. Remove. Add garlic, onion, capsicum and zucchini to camp oven and cook for 2-3 minutes.

Add chopped tomatoes with juice, chicken stock and rice. Bring to boil then simmer with lid on until liquid is absorbed and rice is cooked.

Stir in chicken and peas – if using dried peas add prior to all liquid is absorbed. Cook for a further 5 minutes or until warmed through.

Add a pinch of dried basil and parsley if available and stir through.

jackaroo's rabbit stew

Cooking time: 1 hour 30 minutes. Serves 6

Heat oil in camp oven and add rabbit pieces, cook until browned.

Add onions, bacon, beer, herbs and salt and pepper. Bring to the boil. Move to lower heat and simmer covered for 45 minutes.

Add potatoes and tomatoes and mix well. Cover and simmer for 30 minutes until meat is cooked and potatoes tender.

Mix together the flour and water and stir into stew. Cook for another 2 minutes for sauce to thicken and heat through.

Oil

1 rabbit, cut into pieces

2 onions, sliced

2 bacon rashers, diced

2 cups beer

1 ½ teaspoons dried rosemary

½ teaspoon dried basil

2 potatoes, peeled and cubed

1x410g can tomatoes, chopped

2 tablespoons plain flour

¼ cup water

Salt and pepper to taste

underground mutton casserole

Cooking time: 1 hour 45 minutes. Serves 4-6

Cover rabbit pieces with seasoned flour, shake off excess.

Fry onion and bacon in oil or butter in camp oven until tender. Add rabbit, drained peas, carrot and chicken noddle soup to camp oven. Pour over water.

Bake in camp oven until rabbit is cooked, about 1 to 1½ hours.

1 rabbit cut into 6-8 pieces

2 tablespoons flour seasoned with salt and pepper

1 onion, sliced

4 bacon rashers, chopped

1 cup tinned peas

1 carrot, sliced

1 packet chicken noodle soup

3 cups water

camp oven pizza

Pizzas in the camp oven are easy to make. You have the choice of using home made pizza bases (see page 100 for Pizza Dough recipe), using pita or Lebanese bread or store bought pizza bases. If you don't have any pizza sauce tomato paste is a good replacement sprinkled with some mixed herbs or some oregano and garlic.

Pizza base

Pizza sauce

Grated mozzarella cheese

Toppings to taste

Herbs and spices

Cover pizza base with pizza sauce, toppings and cheese.

Place prepared pizza on a tray and place on trivet in camp oven.

Place most of the hot coals on the lid and only a small amount under the camp oven and cook until the pizza base is crispy and your pizza topping has heated through and the cheese is golden.

Tip ~ If you don't have a camp oven, pizzas can be made just as easily in a heavy based frying pan. Place the prepared pizza into a greased frying pan and cover with the lid or aluminium foil. To ensure that the base does not burn place pan over low coals or on a grate above coals.

One of Cath's famous camp oven pizzas.

satay chicken and banana pizza

Fry chicken strips in oil until cooked. Remove from heat and drain off any liquid.

Pour satay sauce over chicken until well coated.

Mix a little satay sauce with pizza sauce. Spread pizza base with pizza/satay sauce.

Sprinkle thin layer of grated cheese over sauce. Arrange onion, mushrooms, banana and cooked chicken on top. Sprinkle with more cheese.

Bake in camp oven until base is crispy and cheese has melted and turned golden brown.

Tip ~ People question the combination of satay chicken and banana, but it's delicious. Try it for yourself.

Chicken breast or thighs, cut into strips
1 bottle or tin of satay sauce
Pizza base
Pizza sauce
Banana, sliced
Mushrooms, sliced
Onion, sliced
Grated mozzarella or pizza cheese

nachos

Cooking time: 10 minutes

Spread a layer of corn chips on a foil lined baking tray then sprinkle with grated cheese and a little chilli powder.

Spread either salsa or taco sauce over the top. Sprinkle more grated cheese over the top.

Place in camp oven on trivet and bake on hot coals until cheese melts and heated through.

Serve topped with avocado dip and sour cream.

Tip ~ Refried beans can also be added.

Corn chips
Grated cheese
Chilli powder
Salsa or taco sauce
Avocado dip
Sour cream

stockman's egg and bacon pie

Cooking time: 30 minutes. Serves 3 to 4

Combine beaten eggs, milk and flour. Mix well.

Add bacon, cheese and onion. Season with salt and pepper and pour mixture into pie plate.

Place on trivet in camp oven and bake over medium coals until set.

4 eggs, beaten
½ cup self-raising flour
1 ½ cups milk
4 bacon rashers, chopped
1 cup grated cheese
1 onion, finely diced

easy minestrone soup

Cooking time: 20 minutes. Serves 4

1 tablespoon oil	Heat oil in camp oven over hot coals. Add onion and capsicum and cook until tender.
1 onion, finely chopped	
1 capsicum, chopped	Add next five ingredients and bring to the boil.
1x140g tub tomato paste	
4 cups water	Place oven on grate over coals and simmer away for 15 minutes until pasta is just cooked.
1 vegetable stock cube	
1 tablespoon Italian herbs	Add drained tins of mixed vegetables and butter beans and heat through.
½ cup small pasta	
1x440g can mixed vegetables	Tip ~ This quick and easy soup is delicious served with some crusty bread or freshly made damper on a cold winter's day for lunch or dinner.
1x310g can butter beans	

spuds in their jackets

Cooking time: 30-45 minutes

PER PERSON	Pierce potatoes all over with a fork and rub with oil. Place in well oiled camp oven, cover and place in medium to hot coals on base and lid.
Potatoes	
Oil	
Filling of choice	Cook potatoes for 30-45 minutes.
SUGGESTED TOPPINGS/ FILLINGS	Remove from camp oven. Cut a cross in the top of the potato and squeeze the sides to open out.
Butter and cracked black pepper	
Sour cream and chives	Top with your favourite topping/filling.
Grated cheese with finely chopped ham/bacon and chopped spring onions	Tip ~ For those that don't have a camp oven, pierce potatoes all over with a fork, rub with oil and wrap in aluminium foil. Place potatoes in the camp fire coals for about 1½ to 2 hours until cooked.
Mushrooms in butter	
Heated left overs	
Left over Outback Chilli or Bolognaise Sauce	
Heated creamed corn	
Heated baked beans	

yum yum 'tatoes

Cooking time: 30-40 minutes. Serves 4-6 people

Roughly cut potatoes and boil until just tender, drain.

Fry onion and garlic in a little oil or butter until tender. Add chopped bacon and sliced mushrooms and fry until bacon is cooked. Add chopped potatoes and gently mix well.

Place in camp oven or dish in camp oven. Sprinkle grated cheese on top. Bake in camp oven with medium coals on bottom and hot coals on top until cheese is melted and turns golden.

4-6 large potatoes

1 onion, chopped

6 bacon rashers, chopped

1 garlic clove, crushed

1 cup grated cheese

½ cup mushrooms, sliced

stuffed pumpkin

Cooking time: 2 hours. Serves 6 to 8

Place pumpkin in foil lined camp oven. Bake over moderate coals until tender, approx 1 hour. Remove from oven and allow to cool.

Carefully cut top off pumpkin and remove seeds, do not remove flesh. Combine rice, bacon, spring onions, tomatoes, herbs, salt and pepper to taste. Mix well and spoon mixture into pumpkin shell.

Return pumpkin to camp oven. Pour chicken stock over pumpkin filling and replace pumpkin top.

Place camp oven over coals and cook for 30 minutes or until filling is hot and pumpkin flesh is completely cooked.

Tip ~ Individual golden nugget pumpkins could be used.

1 large pumpkin

3-4 cups cooked rice

3 cooked bacon rashers, chopped

6 spring onions, chopped

2-3 tomatoes, chopped

Mixed herbs to taste

Salt and pepper

¼ cup chicken stock

SPIT ROASTING

Spit roasting is an great alternative to cooking roasts in the camp oven. Portable spits are readily available, or if you're handy, are easy to make. With the following recipes you'll become a devotee.

Spit roasting offers an easy and delicious cooking alternative in your camp kitchen. You can expect to get tender, moist, juicy meat. This is due to the direct heat method of cooking and the meat self-basting whilst continually rotating.

Many years ago Craig made a portable spit, which consists of two posts with brackets welded to them, to hold the spit rod and motor. The posts have a tee piece on the top to help with knocking them into the ground with a hammer. The spit rod is a length of stainless steel with a small section of square stainless steel welded to one end which fits into the drive of the spit motor.

The spit is powered by a small rotisserie motor that runs on a two D size batteries. These motors are available from most barbecue shops. The food is held in place on the spit rod by a couple of rotisserie prongs which are also available from barbecue stores.

There are a number of Australian made portable spit roasting units available, two being the *Auspit (pictured opposite)* and the *Aussie Porta Spit*. Both of these units come complete with spit bar, rotisserie motor, meat skewers/prongs and stand.

Try a spit roast as a change from camp oven roasts.

heat source

For spit roasting, a good, consistent heat source is required. The two main heat sources are coals and head beads or briquettes. Both need to be started in plenty of time prior to cooking

If using coals allow at least 1-2 hours to get a good supply of coals from your fire. It is also a good idea to have a small cooking fire nearby so you will have a constant supply of hot coals. This is important when roasting lamb or beef which have cooking times of a couple of hours.

If possible try to avoid positioning your cooking spit where it will be effected by the wind. This will add considerably to the cooking time. If it is windy rig up some form of windbreak.

For a different flavour to your meat, you can add flavoured wood chips to your heat source. These wood chips can be purchased through barbecue and outdoor retailers.

securing food

When spit roasting it is important to ensure that the food is well secured to the spit rod. Skewer the meat with the spit rod, then secure it with the meat prongs and tighten these to the spit rod. If the meat is loose and moves around the rod, or there are pieces of meat hanging, use butcher's string to further secure the meat.

Food must be well balanced on the spit rod to ensure even cooking and to prevent alternating speeds from the motor. When using cuts of meat with a bone, such as a leg of lamb etc, push the spit rod through the meat directly next to the bone on the meatiest side, to give good balance.

To check if the food is well balanced, place tip of spit rod on the ground and spin to see if there is any roll over.

Once the food is ready to be cooked, place the spit rod about 15-20cm above the heat for the first 15 minutes or so to sear the outside and seal in the juices. After this move the rod to a higher setting and cook until the juices flow clear.

cooking times

Cooking times will vary depending on the weight and type of food being cooked and how you prefer your meat cooked. The quality of the heat source and weather conditions will also effect the cooking times.

Use the times below as a guide only:

Chicken	1-1½ hours
Lamb	45 minutes per 500g
Beef	45 - 50 minutes per 500g
Pork	45 - 55 minutes per 500g

spit roasting beef, lamb and pork

Insert spit rod through centre of the meat, if using a piece with a bone, insert through meat beside the bone.

Meats can be glazed, marinated, or make some slits in the meat and insert slivers of garlic and your favourite herb, or just enjoy the delightful smokey flavour of spit roasting.

Spit roast meat over heat source until the meat is cooked to your desired doneness.

Piece of meat
Beef - try silverside
Lamb - leg with bone, boned leg or shoulder
Pork - leg or rolled loin

spit roast beef & red wine

Insert spit rod through centre of the piece of beef and secure with prongs.

Place over heat source and spit roast until cooked as desired.

Combine melted butter, wine, salt and good amount of black pepper and baste beef regularly marinade during cooking.

2kg piece of beef
¼ cup melted butter
½ cup red wine
Ground black pepper
Salt

greek style spit roast lamb

Thoroughly rub lemon over meat, squeezing juice and pulp into meat. Then rub oregano over meat. Let meat marinate in fridge overnight if possible.

Insert spit rod through centre of the lamb leg along the bone and secure with prongs. Season with salt and pepper.

Cook over heat source, regularly brushing with oil, until cooked as desired.

2kg leg of lamb
2 lemons, halved
1 teaspoon dried oregano
¼ cup olive oil
Salt and pepper

spit roast pork loin

Cut one garlic clove into slivers. Cut slits all over pork and insert slivers of garlic along with some rosemary leaves.

Crush the second garlic clove and combine with the balance of rosemary, salt, pepper and the oil. Rub this mixture all over the pork. Let marinate in the fridge for at least 2 to 3 hours.

Remove meat from fridge at least 30 mintues prior to cooking and secure onto spit rod with prongs.

Cook over heat source, brushing with the red wine every 20 minutes, until meat is cooked as desired.

2kg rolled pork loin
2 cloves garlic
2 teaspoons of rosemary
2 teaspoons olive oil
Salt and pepper
1 ½ cups red wine

spit roasting chicken

1 large chicken
little butter or margarine
salt and pepper to taste

When spit roasting chicken tie the legs together securely with string and tie string around the parson's nose so that legs and back are neatly shaped to the bird.

Place a knob of butter and a sprig of parsley in the body cavity. If stuffing, fill loosely into the chicken and truss. With a skewer secure wings and flap over body cavity to enclose stuffing.

Secure the chicken to the spit rod and place over heat source.

Whilst cooking brush chicken with melted butter and sprinkle with salt or seasoning of choice. Or use one of the suggested glazes or rub opposite.

Tip ~ Chicken can become dry during spit roasting, securing strips of bacon over the breast can help alleviate this.

fiery spit roast chicken

1 large chicken
MARINADE
½ cup olive oil
¼ cup lemon juice
¼ cup orange juice
¼ cup red wine vinegar
2-3 tablespoons of Tabasco sauce or piri-piri sauce
2 teaspoons paprika
½ teaspoon ground cumin
4 garlic cloves, crushed
2 teaspoons of ginger
2 teaspoons thyme, fresh is best
1 tablespoon parsley, fresh is best
Salt and pepper to taste

Rinse the chicken and pat dry with paper towel and tie legs and parson's nose.

In large bowl combine all marinade ingredients and mix well. Reserve about a ¼ cup of the marinade.

Place chicken in bowl and turn to coat with marinade. Cover and refrigerate for at least 2 hours, turning chicken a few times.

Remove from fridge 30 minutes prior to cooking.

Secure chicken on spit rod and place over heat source. Spit roast for about 1 ½ hours or until juices run clear. Baste regularly with reserved marinade during cooking.

additional flavours

For some added flavour to your spit roast meat, try out one of these easy to make dry rubs or glazes. These can also be used for your camp oven roast or even for your barbecue meat.

chicken dry rub

1 tablespoon chilli powder

1 tablespoon ground cumin

2 teaspoons dried oregano

2 teaspoons garlic powder

1 teaspoon onion powder

1 teaspoon dry mustard

1 teaspoon sweet paprika

1 teaspoon salt

½ teaspoon ground cayenne pepper

Mix all ingredients together. Brush chicken all over with oil. Rub the dry rub all over chicken thoroughly.

orange honey glaze for chicken

1 cup orange juice

¾ cup honey

1 teaspoon Worcestershire sauce

Mix ingredients and heat in small saucepan. Brush over chichen while on the spit.

ginger honey glaze for chicken

½ cup soy sauce

⅓ cup honey

2 teaspoons ground ginger

Mix ingredients and heat in small saucepan. Brush over chicken while on the spit.

all purpose dry rub

1 tablespoon dried basil

1 tablespoon dried thyme

1 tablespoon dried oregano

2 teaspoons dried rosemary

1 teaspoon salt

½ teaspoon ground pepper

Mix all ingredients together. Brush meat all over with oil. Rub the dry rub all over meat thoroughly. This rub is ideal for beef, lamb, pork and chicken.

lamb dry rub

1 tablespoon dried marjoram

1 dried thyme

2 teaspoons dried oregano

2 teaspoons dried roesmary

1 teaspoon dried sage

½ teaspoon crushed fennel seeds

½ teaspoon salt

½ teaspoon ground pepper

Mix all ingredients together. Brush meat all over with oil. Rub the dry rub vigorously all over meat.

pork dry rub

2 teaspoons dried thyme

2 teaspoons ground allspice

1 teaspoon onion powder

1 teaspoon sugar

½ teaspoon grated nutmeg

½ teaspoon curry powder

½ teaspoon salt

¼ teaspoon ground cinnamon

¼ teaspoon cayenne pepper

pinch ground cloves

Mix all ingredients together. Brush meat all over with oil. Rub the dry rub vigorously all over meat.

SMOKING

For those who haven't tasted the delights of freshly smoked food in the outdoors, these recipes will have your mouth watering in anticipation.

Smoking is a cooking method that seems to be increasing in popularity, even more so now with a number of portable smoke ovens on the market.

These ovens generally use the 'hot' smoking process where the food is placed in the smoking chamber on racks. A layer of sawdust is placed in the bottom of the oven and heat, usually from a spirit burner, is applied to the base of the oven.

You can also use your camp oven to smoke food. Just use the same process as outlined above. However, place your camp oven over the fire instead of a spirit burner.

A word of warning…make sure the sawdust you use for smoking is free of contaminates. The best bet is to use sawdust that is especially packaged for smoking.

When smoking, the ovens produce high temperatures, so ensure that the oven is placed on a solid, heat resistant surface. And always use gloves to open the oven.

Portable smoke ovens are a great way to cook a variety of different foods.

what to smoke?

Many types of food can be smoked including sausages, chicken, eggs, beef, lamb and even nuts, with fish and prawns probably the most popular. The following recipes will give you an insight into cooking with a smoke oven. Most smoke ovens come with a recipe and hints book.

There are some suggestions that foods such as fish and chicken should be soaked in a brine mixture to help keep their moisture, however it is very much a personal preference. If you do wish to use the brine method, a good basic brine mixture can be made of 500 mls of water with 3 tablespoons of salt and 1-2 tablespoons of brown sugar. Soak the food for 15 minutes, take out and pat dry with paper towel, then smoke.

smoking times

As a rough guide foods such as fish, king prawns and most other seafood takes around 15 minutes to smoke with chicken legs, sausages and meat cuts requiring about 25-30 minutes cooking. A cup of methylated spirits will burn for 25-30 minutes.

chicken legs or wings

Cooking Time: 20-25 minutes

Legs or wings per person
1 cup of wine (red or white)
1 tablespoon honey
1 tablespoon soy sauce
1 garlic, clove crushed (optional)

Place all ingredients in a bowl and leave to marinate for at least an hour.

Sprinkle 2 tablespoons of sawdust in smoker.

Place chicken pieces on rack in smoker and smoke until cooked - about 20 minutes.

smoked lamb chops

Cooking Time: 20-25 minutes

Lamb chops of choice
Herb or spice of choice: eg: rosemary, steak spice or one of the McCormick Gourmet Grill & BBQ seasonings would be ideal

Rub both sides of chops with seasoning of choice.

Sprinkle 2 tablespoons of sawdust in smoker.

Place on rack in smoker and smoke for 20 minutes until cooked through.

Tip ~ This could be done with pork chops and chicken breasts.

smoked prawns

Cooking Time: 15-20 minutes

Green prawns, peeled and deveined
Wooden skewers, to fit smoker
Marinade or sauce of choice

Thread prawns onto wooden skewers.

Place prawn skewers in shallow dish and cover with sauce and marinate until ready to cook.

Sprinkle 2 tablespoons of sawdust in smoker.

Place skewers on rack in smoker and smoke for 15 minutes.

smoked trout

Cooking Time: 15-20 minutes

Gutted trout
Melted butter
Dried mixed herbs
Squeeze of lemon juice

Combine melted butter, mixed herbs and lemon juice. Brush inside of trout with the mixture.

Sprinkle 2 tablespoons of sawdust in smoker.

Place trout on rack in smoker and smoke for 20 minutes until tender.

smoked chicken breasts

Cooking Time: 20 minutes

Sprinkle 2 tablespoon on sawdust in smoker. Place chicken breasts on rack and smoke for 20 minutes.

Chicken breasts

These smoked breasts are great sliced in a salad or used in a cream and seeded mustard sauce (fry diced onion and garlic in a little oil, add some cream or evaporated milk to pan with tablespoon of seeded mustard, simmer over low heat, add sliced smoked chicken breast and heat through, great over pasta).

smoked ribs

Cooking Time: 20-30 minutes

Sprinkle 2 tablespoons on sawdust in smoker. Brush ribs with sauce, such as a smokey barbecue sauce or sweet and sour sauce, leave to marinate until ready to cook. Place pork ribs on rack and smoke for 20-30 minutes.

Pork spare ribs

smoked eggs

Cooking Time: 15 minutes

Sprinkle 2 tablespoons of sawdust in smoker. Place shelled, boiled eggs on smoker rack. Smoke for 15 mintues until a pale golden colour.

Boiled eggs

Enjoy these hot or cold, either by themselves seasoned with salt and pepper, on sandwiches, as part of a ploughmans lunch or an antipasto platter.

ham steaks & pineapple

Cooking Time: 20 minutes

Want a twist to your ham steaks and pineapple? Smoke them instead of barbecuing.

Ham steaks
Pineapple rings

Sprinkle 2 tablespoon on sawdust in smoker. Place ham steaks and pineapple rings on rack. Smoke for 20 minutes.

smoked snags

Cooking Time: 20 minutes

Sprinkle 2 tablespoons on sawdust in smoker. Place sausages on rack and smoke for approximately 20 minutes.

Sausages

SALADS AND VEGETABLES

These tasty salad and vegetable recipes make the perfect accompaniment to any meat, fish or poultry dish. It really is easy being green.

new chums pasta salad

Serves 4

Combine oil, lemon juice and salt and pepper in a jar and mix well.

While pasta is still hot pour over dressing. Allow to cool.

Once cooled, add vegetables and toss well.

Tip ~ Use ½ a cup of your favourite salad dressing instead.

2-3 cups of hot cooked pasta
1 cup corn kernels
4 shallots, chopped
1 capsicum, chopped
½ cup oil
¼ cup lemon juice
Salt and black pepper

corn salad

Serves 4

Combine corn and capsicum.

For the dressing, combine all ingredients in a screw top jar and shake well to combine.

Pour dressing over corn and capsicum.

1x420g tin of corn, drained
1 red capsicum, sliced
1 green capsicum, sliced
DRESSING
⅓ cup mayonnaise
1 tablespoon lemon juice
½ teaspoon ground cumin

bean salad

Serves 4

Mix all vegetables together and pour over your favourite salad dressing.

1x430g can 3 Bean Mix, drained and rinsed
1 onion, sliced
1 capsicum, sliced
2 tomatoes, diced

pesto potato salad

Serves 4

Boil potatoes until just tender.

Whilst boiling, mix mayonnaise and pesto together.

Stir mayonnaise mixture through cooked potatoes until well covered.

3 large potatoes, peeled and cubed
½ cup mayonnaise
1 tablespoon bottled pesto

rice salad

Serves 4

2-3 cups cooked rice
1 capsicum, chopped
4 shallots, chopped
1x310g can corn kernels, drained
Salt and pepper to season
1x450g can pineapple pieces, drained
$1/3$ cup sultanas
DRESSING
$1/3$ cup oil
2 tablespoons lemon juice
$1/4$ teaspoon dry mustard
$1/4$ teaspoon sugar

Combine rice with vegetables and fruit. Season with salt and pepper.

Dressing, mix all ingredients in small screw top jar and shake well to mix. Pour dressing over salad and toss well.

Tip ~ Use 1 cup of store bought French Salad Dressing as an alternative.

curried pasta salad

Serves 4

2 cups of cooked pasta
1 capsicum, chopped
4 shallots, chopped
1 cup celery, sliced
1 cup mushrooms, sliced
CURRY DRESSING
2 tablespoons brown sugar
2 tablespoons curry powder
$1/2$ cup oil
$1/2$ cup white vinegar

Combine pasta and vegetables in bowl and mix well.

Curry dressing, combine all ingredients in a small screw top jar and shake to mix well.

Pour dressing over salad.

Tip ~ A tablespoon of cream can be added to the curry dressing.

couscous salad

Serves 4

Place couscous and boiling water in boil. Let stand for 5 minutes until water is absorbed. Fluff couscous with a fork.

Add remaining ingredients and mix well to combine.

This is great served with Tandoori lamb cutlets, see page 31.

1 ½ cups couscous
1 ½ cups boiling water
⅓ cup dried currants
2 teaspoons grated lemon rind
2 teaspoons lemon juice
¼ cup coriander leaves, chopped

thai salad base

Combine all salad ingredients in a bowl or on a serving platter.

Drizzle with dressing.

Tip ~ This is an easy salad base to which some thinly sliced barbecued or stir fried beef or chicken, which have been brushed with a chilli sauce or paste, can be added. Or slice up some smoked chicken breast from page 79. Shredded cabbage can replace the salad leaves.

Mixed salad leaves
Red onion, thinly sliced
Cherry tomatoes, halved
Lebanese cucumber, thinly sliced
Optional - coriander leaves and mint leaves
Kraft Chilli & Lime dressing

gado gado salad

Place carrots and beans in a pot of boiling water for 2 minutes. Drain and refresh with cold water.

Arrange all vegetables on a serving platter with sliced boiled eggs.

Drizzle satay sauce over vegetables.

Tip ~ This is a nice easy salad that looks pretty impressive, and is a great way to use up vegetables. Bean sprouts can also be added.

2 carrots, thinly sliced
Handful of green beans, sliced
1 cup shredded cabbage
1 cucumber, thinly sliced
2 hard boiled eggs
2 spring onions sliced
Bottled satay sauce

vegetable kebabs

Onion wedges
Capsicums
Button mushrooms
Cherry tomatoes or tomato wedges
Eggplant
Zucchini
Pineapple cubes

MARINADE
1 tablespoon oil
1 tablespoon soy sauce
1 tablespoon pineapple juice

Thread vegetables and fruit on skewers.

Combine all marinade ingredients.

Cook on lightly oiled barbecue plate or grill brushing with marinade until vegetables are heated through and tender.

Tip ~ Any mix of vegetables can be used.

vegie patties

Potato, Carrot, Zucchini
Egg
Salt and pepper
Flour

Grate all vegetables. Add egg, seasoning and enough flour to vegetables to make a thick batter.

Spoon vegetable batter onto hot oiled barbecue plate. Cook till brown, turn and cook other side.

Delicious served as a snack or as side dish to barbecue meat.

Tip ~ Use whatever vegetables you may have.

char grilled vegies

Sliced vegetables such as zucchini, egg plant, potato, sweet potato, pumpkin, squash and asparagus can all be char grilled over hot coals.

Potato, sweet potato and pumpkin should be parboiled first until just tender.

Place vegetables on well oiled grill over hot coals. Brush vegetables with oil and grill until tender.

Tip ~ Sprinkle with your favourite seasoning while cooking.

fossickers hot onion salad

Serves 4

Combine all ingredients in a bowl and leave to marinate (the longer the better).

Cook on barbecue plate until onions are soft.

Delicious served with barbecued meat.

3-4 medium sized onions, sliced

1/3 cup oil

1/2 cup red wine

1 tablespoon seeded mustard

2 teaspoons honey

1 teaspoon dried mixed herbs

cheesy potatoes

Serves 4

Cut potatoes in half and place, cut side down, in greased camp oven or greased dish. Sprinkle with pinch of paprika and garlic salt.

Bake in moderate coals until potatoes are tender, approximately 40 mintues.

Cover potatoes with cheese slices, brush with melted butter. Cook in coals with coals on lid until cheese has melted, approximately 7-10 minutes.

Tip ~ For a change place strips of bacon, ham, smoked salmon, onion or tomato on the potatoes before placing the cheese on top.

4 large potatoes, peeled

Pinch of paprika

Pinch of garlic salt

4-5 cheese slices

1 tablespoon melted butter

pan fried potatoes and bacon

Serves 4

Boil potatoes until just tender. Drain and place potatoes in a bowl.

Combine flour, shallots and cream. Mix cream mixture with potatoes.

Cook bacon until crispy in frying pan.

Pour potato mixture on top of bacon and cook until potato mixture browns on the bottom. Turn mixture over and brown other side.

Tip ~ This tasty recipe is ideal to use up left over boiled potatoes.

3 medium sized potatoes, peeled and diced

1 tablespoon plain flour

2 shallots, chopped

1/4 cup cream

2 bacon rashers, finely chopped

DESSERTS AND CAKES

An evening meal in the outdoors without a tempting dessert to finish is like a meat pie without sauce—they just go together! Try a few of these recipes and you'll know what we mean.

honey cinnamon bananas

Place peeled bananas on the foil square and slice lengthways down the middle of banana. Do not cut the whole way through.

Drizzle honey in the cut and sprinkle cinnamon sugar over honey.

Wrap foil around the banana tightly and place on grill over fire. Turning over once or twice. Cook until bananas are warmed through and soft.

Carefully open foil and slide bananas into bowl.

Delicious served with custard and/or cream.

Tip ~ For a tasty change replace the honey and cinnamon with pieces of chocolate and marshmallow.

Bananas
Honey
Cinnamon sugar
Foil squares to fit bananas

creamy coconut bananas

Cooking time: 5 minutes. Serves 4

Warm coconut milk, honey and a sprinkle of vanilla in a saucepan. Stir until the honey has dissolved.

Add sliced bananas. Bring to the boil and stir for about 1 minute.

Serve hot or cold.

3–4 bananas, peeled and sliced
2 tablespoons honey
1 cup coconut milk
Vanilla essence

rummy fruits

Cooking time: 10-15 minutes. Serves 4

Place apricots, prunes, raisins, orange juce and cinnamon stick in pan. Bring to boil and simmer for 10 minutes.

Add bananas and simmer for a further 2 minutes.

Add rum and stir through.

Serve with custard, creamed rice or the rice pudding on page 91.

12 dried apricots
12 dried prunes
½ cup raisins or sultanas
1 cup orange juice
1 cinnamon stick
4 bananas, peeled and thickly sliced
1-2 tablespoons of rum

desserts and cakes

fruity kebabs

Fruit of choice, either fresh or tinned such as: pineapple, apple, mango, kiwi fruit, peach, banana, etc

2 tablespoons honey

Juice of 1 lemon

2 tablespoons of favourite spirit: brandy, rum or malibu is good - optional

Combine honey, lemon juice and spirit if using.

Cook kebabs on lightly oiled grill or hot plate, brushing with marinade.

Tip ~ If serving these to the kids, best to leave the spirit out!

lemon banana pancakes

10 large basic pancakes

½ cup mashed banana

½ cup thickened cream

1 tablespoon lemon juice

1 tablespoon caster sugar

Prepare pancakes, see basic pancake mix on page 27, and keep warm wrapped in foil to side of fire.

Mix banana, cream, lemon juice and sugar together. Spread mixture liberally on pancakes.

Roll up and sprinkle with a little extra caster sugar.

cocky's joy dumplings

1 cup self-raising flour

1 tablespoond butter

1 egg

Milk

1 egg

SYRUP

1 cup water

1 cup sugar

1 tablespoon butter

1 tablespoon golden syrup

SYRUP

Add all ingredients into camp oven or large saucepan and bring to the boil.

DUMPLINGS

Rub butter into flour until it resembles bread crumbs.

Add egg and enough milk to make dough.

Roll dough into small balls and drop into boiling syrup. Cover and boil dumplings in syrup for 20 minutes.

Serve dumplings with syrup poured over and custard or cream.

Tip ~ Instead of boiling, these dumplings can be baked. Place dumplings in a dish or directly into camp oven, pour syrup mixture oven and bake in moderate coals for 20 minutes.

bread 'n butter pudding

Cooking time: 45-50 minutes. Serves 4-6

Remove crusts from bread and spread one side with butter and jam. Cut into fingers or squares.

Place a layer of bread, butter and jam side up, in a lightly buttered tin or dish or straight into the camp oven. Sprinkle with sultanas or apricots if using.

Place second layer of bread, butter and jam side down on top of first layer.

Beat eggs, sugar, milk and vanilla together. Pour egg mixture over bread and let stand for 15 minutes while the bread absorbs all liquid.

Sprinkle with some nutmeg.

Bake in camp oven with medium coals on base and on lid for 45 minutes or until the top is browned.

Tip ~ This is a great way of using up that stale bread!

8-10 slices of stale bread
4 eggs
2 cups milk
¼ cup sugar
Jam of choice
Butter
1 teaspoon vanilla essence, optional
3 tablespoons sultanas or chopped dried apricots, optional
Nutmeg

apple crumble

Cooking time: 30 minutes. Serves 4-6

Mix together flour, sugar, cinnamon and butter until it resembles bread crumbs.

Place apples in pie dish and cover with flour mixture.

Bake in camp oven with medium coals on bottom and hotter coals on top, for 25-30 minutes until top is golden.

Tip ~ For a different taste sprinkle a hand full of sultanas over the apples or use peaches sprinkled with some crushed cloves.

1x800g can tinned apple
1 cup self-raising flour
½ cup brown sugar
½ teaspoon cinnamon
½ cup butter

rockleigh apples

Serves 4

Cook apples in orange juice, sugar and cinnamon and port if using until just tender.

Serve apples with warm liquid and custard or cream. This is a great no fuss dessert.

4 apples, peeled, cored and sliced
1 cup orange juice
3 tablespoons raw sugar
1 teaspoon cinnamon
Port, optional

dungaree settlers baked apples

Cooking time: 30-40 minutes. Serves 6

6 large green cooking apples
2 tablespoons of chopped dates
2 tablespoons of sultanas
1 teaspoon cinnamon
½ teaspoon ground cloves
Brown sugar
Butter

Core apples. Slice through the peel around the apple about half way down a couple of times. This will stop the apples from bursting.

Mix together dates, sultanas, cinnamon and ground cloves. Fill apple centres with date mixture.

Sprinkle top of apples with brown sugar and dot with butter.

Bake on tray or foil in camp oven, over medium coals, until apples are soft. Around 30 minutes depending on coals.

Serve with custard and cream.

paroo peach pie

Cooking time: 20-30 minutes. Serves 4-6

1x825g can sliced peaches, drained
2 tablespoons butter
½ sugar (caster if you have some)
Teaspoon vanilla essence
1 egg
1 cup self-raising flour
½ cup milk
¼ desiccated coconut

Arrange peaches over base of a pie dish.

Cream butter, sugar and vanilla together and gradually beat in the egg. Add dry ingredients and milk. Mix until smooth.

Spread mixture over the peaches and sprinkle with extra coconut. Bake in camp oven until golden and top is set.

Serve hot with custard.

murrah pudding

Serves 4

1-2 slices stale white bread per person
½ cup milk
1 teaspoon white sugar
1 egg yolk, lightly beaten
Butter for frying
Jam of choice, heated

Cut crusts from bread.

Combine milk and sugar. Dip bread into milk mixture.

Drain bread then dip into egg yolk.

Heat butter in frying pan or on barbecue plate. Fry bread on both sides until golden brown.

Serve with hot jam poured over each slice.

silver city lemon pudding

Grease a pie dish that fits into camp oven.

In a large bowl beat together flour, butter, sugar, eggs and lemon rind. Best to use a wooden spoon for this.

Gradually add milk to make a smooth consistency.

Spread mixture into pie dish. Pour sauce over the top.

Bake in camp oven on trivet over hot coals for 30-35 minutes or when the mixture is golden and firm on top.

SAUCE

Combine lemon juice and boiling water to make 1¼ cup of liquid.

Mix together the sugar and cornflour. Gradually add the lemon juice mixture to the cornflour. Mix well.

¾ cup self-raising flour
3 tablespoons butter, softened
¾ cup caster sugar
2 eggs
Grated rind of 1 lemon
1-2 tablespoons milk
SAUCE
¾ caster sugar
2 tablespoons cornflour
Juice of 1 lemon
Boiling water

rice pudding

Serves 4

Use a 4 cup capacity dish that fits in camp oven.

Brush dish with melted butter. Place rice in dish. Sprinkle sugar, sultanas and orange rind over rice, then pour the milk over.

Place dish in heated camp oven and bake in slow coals for 1¾ hours.

Combine cimmamon and sugar. Sprinkle over pudding and bake for a further 20 minutes until pudding is firm.

Tip ~ We enjoy this pudding with the rummy fruits on page 87.

½ cup medium or short grain rice
1 tablespoon soft brown sugar
2 tablespoons sultanas
1 teaspoon grated orange rind
3 cups milk
½ teaspoon ground cinnamon
2 teaspoons soft brown sugar

ginger cream log

250g Ginger Nut biscuits

1x400g can crushed pineapple drained, juice reserved

1x300ml carton cream, whipped

1 tablespoon brandy or rum, optional

Mix pineapple with half the whipped cream.

Place the biscuits in a log shape on a large piece of foil. Spread the cream and pineapple mixture on the biscuits, pressing them   against each other keeping the biscuits in a log shape.

Sprinkle with 1 tablespoon of reserved juice and your choice of spirit.

Roll the foil up tightly around the log and chill overnight.

To serve place the log on a serving plate and cover with the remaining whipped cream.

Tip ~ This dessert log is delicious. The only real effort to make this is whipping the cream – if you have the patience to do this by hand whilst at camp you will definitely enjoy this dessert.

rouseabouts cake

2 cups dried mixed fruit

1 ¼ cups brown sugar

1 cup strong black tea

1 egg, lightly beaten

4 tablespoons golden syrup

4 cups self-raising flour

1 teaspoon mixed spice, cinnamon, nutmeg, cloves

Place fruit and brown sugar in bowl and pour tea over. Cover and let stand overnight.

Grease cake tin and/or line with baking paper if you have it.

Combine egg, golden syrup, flour and spice to the fruit and tea. Mix well. Spoon mixture into prepared tin and place on trivet inside camp oven.

Bake in camp oven for 1 to 1½ hours with medium hot coals on the base and on lid.

jam roly-poly

Cooking time: 30-40 minutes. Serves 4-6

2 cups self-raising flour

Pinch salt

3 tablespoons butter

Pinch of salt

Water

¾ cup jam, apricot is delicious

½ cup sultanas, optional

1 teaspoon melted butter

Mix flour and salt togther in a bowl and rub in butter. Slowly add enough water to make a dough.

On lightly floured surface, roll dough out into a thin rectangle.

Spread jam on dough lengthways, if using sultanas sprinkle over jam. Roll dough up lengthways.

Place roll into a greased pie dish, loaf tin or plate. Using a sharp knife make a few slits in the top of roll and lightly spread with melted butter.

Bake in camp oven with medium coals on bottom and hot coals on top for about 30 to 40 minutes.

Serve hot with custard or whipped cream.

dried fruit salad

This is best made in the morning so it can stand during the day for the fruit to swell to be ready for dessert that evening or alternatively make it in the evening and leave over night to be ready for breakfast the following morning.

Place dried fruit in a bowl and cover with fresh tea. Leave to stand for the day or overnight.

Add lemon juice and honey or sugar to taste, mix well.

Serve with custard for an easy dessert or yoghurt for a delicious breakfast.

500g mixed dried fruits (apples, peaches, sultanas, apricots, etc)
1 ½ cups hot unsweetened tea
Juice of 1 lemon
Honey or sugar to taste

no bake biccies

Makes about 60 biccies.

In large saucepan mix together sugar and cocoa powder. Add milk and butter.

Over high heat add oats, coconut and walnuts. Mix well.

Quickly drop rounded teaspoonfuls of mixture onto greaseproof paper.

Allow 1 hour to set.

2 cups white sugar
1/3 cup cocoa powder
½ cup milk
125g butter
3 cups rolled oats
1 ½ cups shredded coconut
½ cup chopped walnuts

no bake lemon slice

Mix together crushed biscuits and coconut.

Add condensed milk, butter and lemon rind. Mix well.

Press mixture into greased slice/lamington tin and refrigerate for one hour.

LEMON ICING

Place icing sugar in bowl and stir in softened butter.

Mix in enough lemon juice to make the icing a spreadable consistency. Spread over slice.

Cut into slices and enjoy with a cuppa.

1x250g packet of milk arrowroot biscuits, crushed
2/3 cup (200ml) sweetened condensed milk
1 cup desiccated coconut
4 tablespoons butter, melted
Grated rind of 2 lemons
LEMON ICING
1 ½ cups icing sugar
1 teaspoon butter
2 tablespoon lemon juice – approximately

DAMPER, BREAD, SCONES AND MUFFINS

Man can't live on bread alone—so we've included recipes for delicious dampers, scones and muffins as well as breads that are easy to bake in your bush kitchen.

damper

During the early days of European settlement in Australia, bush travellers survived mainly on tea and damper. The tea could have been made from tea-tree leaves or sassafras bark and the damper made of plain flour and water, and if supplies were available salt could have been added. The flour and water was mixed into a dough and shaped into a flat circle about six centimetres thick, then placed in a hole made in the hot ashes of the camp fire. More ashes were moved over the top to keep air out, to prevent the damper burning. After thirty minutes tiny cracks would appear on the surface from where steam had escaped. The damper was cooked if it sounded hollow when gently tapped with a stick.

In time a rising agent was added to the dough to make it lighter and more digestible. Camp ovens started to be used, protecting the damper from the ashes. Sometimes dripping or lard was used as was milk, sour milk or buttermilk as a substitute for water. Damper variations included Johnny-cakes (small dampers or scones), devil-on-the-coals (pieces of damper cooked quickly on the embers and turned by hand), sinkers (small balls of dough with fat mixed in and then boiled to make dumplings) and leather-jackets (scones fried in whatever fat was available).

Today the traditional damper recipe has been adapted by keen cooks through to campers and bushwalkers with self raising flour used to substitute the need for a rising agent and oil or milk used instead of water.

Damper baked in a camp oven.

damper or bread?

Many people's first thoughts when they purchase a camp oven is about baking mouth-watering dampers dripping with butter and lashings of golden syrup or cocky's joy. Sounds good doesn't it?

Generally, most people—us included, prefer bread to damper. With the advent of pre-packaged bread mixes and the wide availability of bread, even in the outback areas, the time honoured practice of damper making is fast becoming a dying art. We encourage you to help keep this staple alive and well!

swaggies traditional damper

4 cups plain flour	Mix flour and baking soda together.
½ teaspoon baking soda	Make a well in the centre and add water. Mix to a soft dough.
1 ⅓ cups water, approximately	Shape into a flattened cake and cut a cross in the top with a sharp knife.
	Place into greased camp oven, cover and allow to rise for 15 minutes.
	Place camp oven in a hole lined with hot coals, place extra coals on top of camp oven. Depending on heat of coals baking time will vary. Test after 25 minutes. Damper is cooked when a hollow sound is produced when lightly tapped.

basic damper mix

Serves 2

1 cup self raising flour	Mix all ingredients into a firm dough. Shape and lightly dust the outside with flour.
¼ cup milk or water	
Pinch of salt	Place into a greased camp oven and cover. Cook in medium coals, check after 25 minutes.
	Damper is cooked when it has a golden crust and an inserted skewer comes out clean.

variations to the basic damper recipe

savoury: add onion, bacon, grated cheese, sliced olives, capsicum or mixed herbs.

sweet: add honey, jam, sultanas, chocolate chips, nuts or sugar.

dessert damper: shape dough into a long thick snake and twist around a stick. Cook in the camp oven or loosely wrap some foil around it and cook in the coals. When cooked it comes away with a hollow centre. Fill the centre with jam or golden syrup and cream.

decadent: when moulding the dough, place a wedge of camembert or brie cheese in the centre of the damper.

beer damper

4 cups self raising flour	Place flour in bowl. Make a well in the centre and add the butter and beer.
1 tablespoon butter or margarine	
375ml beer	Mix to a soft dough. Add extra flour if needed. Shape dough into a ball and slightly flatten.
	Place on greased tray in camp oven cover and place over medium hot coals, adding coals to lid.
	Bake until well risen and brown. Check after 25 minutes.

ABOVE: *Sausages and eggs (page 79) smoked in a Togar Smoke Oven (page 19). A range of gourmet sausage flavours are smoked here, producing some great smokey flavours — especially good with spicy style sausages.*

RIGHT: *Mexican Quesadillas (page 43) served with sour cream and a sprinkle of paprika.*

BELOW: *Baked Chops with Tomatoes (page 61) dished up with slices of damper made from the Basic Damper Mix (page 96).*

ABOVE: *Tex Mex Burgers (page 36) ready to be served.*

RIGHT: *Craig checking on the spit roasted lamb (page 73) and potatoes on the Australian made portable Auspit (page 20).*

ABOVE: *Camp oven pizza is always a favourite (page 66).*

BELOW: *Chicken Satay Sticks (page 34) are easy to prepare and take little time to cook over hot coals on a grill.*

ABOVE: *Cocky's Joy Dumplings (page 88), boiling in the syrup in a camp oven.*

LEFT: *Tex Mex Burgers (page 36) served in a tortilla ready to be rolled up and enjoyed.*

BELOW LEFT: *A favourite dessert, Rummy Fruits (page 87) served with Rice Pudding (page 91).*

BELOW RIGHT: *An oldie but a goodie, Apple Crumble (page 89) is delicious served with custard.*

easy pumpkin damper

Mix all ingredients together. Knead for a few minutes on a well floured surface.

Shape into damper and place on greased tray. Bake in camp oven for 45-60 minutes until cooked.

1 cup rye flour
1 ½ cups wholemeal flour
1 cup All-Bran
250g sultanas
3 tablespoons honey
1 cup cooked mashed pumpkin
1 ½ cups water drained from cooked pumpkin
Pinch of cinnamon

cheesey damper

Place flour in bowl. Add enough milk to make a sticky dough.

Knead on floured surface and shape into a large round. Press down so dough is about 3cm thick.

Place onto lightly greased tray. With a shape knife mark the round into 10 wedges and cut down 1cm deep.

Combine cheese and mustard and sprinkle over dough.

Place tray into camp oven cover and cook on moderate coals with coals on lid.

Cook until damper is golden brown and sounds hollow when tapped. Check after 30 minutes.

4 cups self raising flour
2 ½ cups milk, approximately
1 cup grated cheese
1 teaspoon mustard powder

pan-fried bread

If you don't have a camp oven you can make your own bread by using a heavy based frying pan — try this pan-fried bread.

Mix all ingredients and knead for a few minutes until dough is rubbery and elastic.

Cover and leave for 30 minutes.

Divide into small balls and pat flat.

Fry bread in a frying pan or on hot plate in hot oil until golden. Drain on paper towels before serving.

3 cups self raising flour
2 tablespoons oil
1 cup warm water

pumpkin and bacon fried bread

1 cup cooked mashed pumpkin

2 bacon rashers, chopped and cooked

1 onion, chopped and cooked

2½ cups self-raising flour

1 egg, beaten

1 tablespoon milk

1 teaspoon dry mustard

¼ teaspoon cayenne pepper

2 tablespoons butter

Stir egg and milk into pumpkin.

Place flour, mustard and cayenne pepper into a bowl and rub in butter. Add bacon, onion and pumpkin mixture to flour. Combine well.

Turn onto floured surface and knead until mixture is smooth. Roll out to a damper shape but about 3cm thick and mark into wedges.

Place into greased frying pan or onto greased barbecue plate. Cook over medium heat, turning a few times during cooking until cooked through, about 30 minutes.

drovers soda bread

3 cups wholemeal flour

1 cup plain white flour

1 teaspoon salt

1 teaspoon bicarbonate of soda

1 tablespoon butter

Approximately 500ml of milk

Mix dry ingredients. Rub butter in with fingers.

Make a well in the centre and gradually add milk, only add enough to make mixture soft, and mix until the dough is spongy.

Turn dough onto floured surface and knead. Shape into a loaf about 5cm thick.

Place on lightly greased tray and brush the top with milk. Slash the top of the dough with a sharp knife about two or three times, this stops the crust cracking.

Bake in camp oven on moderate coals and coals on lid for about 40 minutes. Check halfway through.

scones

2 cups self raising flour

2 teaspoons sugar

½ tablespoon butter

1 cup milk

Combine flour and sugar into bowl and rub butter in with fingers. Make a well in centre, add nearly all the milk, using a knife to cut the milk through the flour mixture making a soft, sticky dough. Add remaining milk if needed.

Roll dough out on a lightly floured surface and knead until smooth.

Press dough out to a 2cm thickness. Cut dough into squares or use a cup to make rounds and place onto a greased baking tray. Brush a little milk on tops of scones.

Place baking tray on trivet in hot camp oven and bake for 10 minutes or until tops are browned and scones sound hollow when tapped.

date scones

Combine dry ingredients in bowl. Add chopped dates. Add egg, cream and lemonade. Mix well.

Roll dough out on a lightly floured surface and knead until smooth.

Press dough out to a 2cm thickness. Cut dough into squares or use a cup to make rounds and place onto a greased baking tray.

Place baking tray on trivet in hot camp oven and bake for 10-15 minutes or until tops are browned and scones sound hollow when tapped.

3 cups self raising flour
1 tablespoon icing sugar
1 egg, beaten
1x300ml carton cream
300ml lemonade
¼ teaspoon salt
1 cup dates, chopped

basic muffin mix

Makes 6 large muffins or 12 small muffins

Place flour and sugar in bowl, add egg and milk. Mix well.

Spoon into greased muffin pan and bake in camp oven with medium coals for about 20-30 minutes. Check after 20 minutes. Muffins are cooked when a skewer comes out clean. Rest muffins in the pan for 5 minutes, then shake out.

Tip ~ I use wholemeal self raising flour as it gives the muffins a great consistency. Grease muffin pan with butter and then sprinkle with a light dusting of flour.

2 cups self raising flour
2 tablespoons soft brown sugar
1 egg
1 cup milk

variations to the basic muffin mix

fruit: add your favourite fruit: grated apple; mashed banana; grated pear; sultanas; berries.

savoury: omit the brown sugar and add: herbs; cooked bacon; cooked onion; grated cheese.

cheese & herb muffins

Place flour, milk powder, salt and pepper into bowl. Using your fingers rub in butter.

Add dried herbs, cheese, eggs and water. Mix well. Spoon into greased muffin tin.

Place muffin tin inside camp oven. Cover and place over medium to hot coals with coals on lid.

Cook for 20 minutes. If not completely cooked, return to heat on base and lid and continue until muffins are well cooked and a skewer comes out clean when inserted.

3 cups self raising flour
½ cup full cream milk powder
Salt and pepper
2 tablespoons butter
1 teaspoon oregano
1 teaspoon dried basil
1 teaspoon dried parsley
1 cup grated tasty cheese
2 eggs, lightly beaten
1 ½ cups water

yoghurt muffins

2 cups self raising flour
½ cup brown sugar
½ teaspoon cinnamon
1 egg, lightly beaten
½ cup milk
200g Fruche yoghurt – with or without fruit
3 mashed bananas or stewed apples

Mix flour, sugar and cinnamon together. Add all other ingredients and mix up lightly.

Spoon into greased 6 large cup muffin pan.

Place muffin pan into camp oven and bake in moderate coals for approximately 30 minutes.

Tip ~ A ½ cup of crushed walnuts or pecans can be added.

pineapple nut bread

2 cups self raising flour
½ teaspoon salt
½ cup sugar
½ cup chopped nuts of choice
1 egg, lightly beaten
3 tablespoons melted butter
1 ½ cup crushed pineapple, well drained
Vanilla essence

Mix together flour, salt and sugar. Stir in nuts. Add egg, melted butter and pineapple. Mix well.

Pour into greased loaf tin. Place in camp oven and bake in moderate coals for an hour, or until a skewer comes out clean.

Serve sliced with butter.

pizza dough

This will make enough dough for two 28cm pizzas

7g sachet dried yeast
½ teaspoon sugar
½ teaspoon salt
1 cup warm water
2 ½ cups plain flour

Combine yeast, sugar, salt and water in bowl. Cover with plastic wrap and stand in warm place until mixture is foamy, around 10 minutes.

Place flour in large bowl and make a well in centre. Add the yeast mixture and mix to a dough.

Knead dough on a floured surface until it becomes smooth and elastic, this should take 5 to 10 minutes.

Roll out to size and thickness. Place on greased tray and top with favourite pizza toppings.

shortcrust pastry

Blend flour and salt together. Mix in butter with fingertips until mixture looks a bit like breadcrumbs.

Slowly add milk or water and mix until there is no dry flour left and becomes a stiff dough.

Knead on floured board until smooth. Roll out to size.

Tip ~ This should make enough to use for base and lid of a 20cm pie dish. For a sweet shortcrust pastry add 1 tablespoon of sugar with flour and salt.

2 cups plain flour
½ teaspoon salt
½ cup milk or water
4 tablespoons butter, softend but not melted

puff pastry

Place flour in bowl and cut in butter.

Mix egg, water and lemon juice together and stir into flour mixture until it forms a ball.

Knead lightly on floured board and roll out.

Fold one side of pastry into the middle, then fold the other side on top of it. Roll flat and make one quarter turn to the left. Repeat the folding, rolling and turning three times.

Rest pastry in a cool place 30 minutes or more before use.

Tip ~ Ideal for pies, sausage rolls and quiches.

250g plain flour
¾ cup butter, in small cubes
1 egg
6 tablespoons cold water
2 teaspoons lemon juice

biscuit pastry

Cream butter and sugar. Add egg and mix well.

Work in flour.

Roll out pastry and cut out shapes. Sprinkle spices like cinnamon on the shapes.

Place on greased tray and bake in moderate to hot camp oven for 15 minutes until cooked.

Tip ~ This pastry is also ideal for a pie base, slice base and jam tarts.

1 egg
½ cup butter
½ cup sugar
2 cups self raising flour

emergency pie base

Crush biscuits finely and mix in melted butter.

Press firmly into base of pie dish. Refrigerate base until firm before using.

Tip ~ Use sweet biscuits for a sweet pie and plain biscuits for a savoury pie base.

2 tablespoons butter
200g plain biscuits

NIBBLIES

Late afternoons relaxing beside the camp fire with a cold beverage in hand is the perfect time to try out some of these nibblies.

cajun oysters

Combine the cajun seasoning, paprika and basil. Mix well. Reserve a teaspoon for serving.

Add flour to spice mix and stir.

Thread oysters onto wooden skewers. Coat with spiced flour mix.

Heat oil on hot plate or in frying pan. Cook oysters until golden, about 6 minutes, turning several times. Drain on paper towel.

Serve with reserved spice mix sprinkled over and your choice of dipping sauce or even mayonnaise.

Tip ~ We always carry tins of smoked oysters whilst travelling and this is a favourite to start off a meal with an icy cold beer. If you're in a position to get fresh oysters even better. Remember don't raid commercial oyster leases as they can tend to get upset, for good reason!

2 tins of smoked oysters or 12 large shelled oysters
1 teaspoon cajun seasoning
¼ teaspoon dried paprika
¼ teaspoon dried basil
¼ cup plain flour
Wooden skewers
Oil or butter to fry

devilled nuts

Heat oil in a frying pan. Fry the nuts one handful at a time. When golden remove and drain on absorbent paper.

When nuts have been fried combine salt and chilli powder and sprinkle over nuts.

When cold dust off excess salt and chilli powder and serve.

Tip ~ These nuts are easy to make whilst at camp or you could make these up before leaving home and store in an airtight container.

500g raw nuts – peanuts, almonds, cashews etc
Oil for frying
2 teaspoons salt
2 teaspoons chilli powder

nuts and bolts

Mix all dry ingredients together.

Pour over warmed oil and mix well.

Cool and store in airtight container.

Tip ~ I love these, the only problem is they are quite moreish. This recipe makes a large quantity, but it does keep well in an airtight container, so could be made before going camping. Or do as our friend does and gives jars of Nuts and Bolts as a gift at Christmas.

300g packet of Nutrigran cereal
375g salted nuts -peanuts or cashews
1 packet cream of chicken soup
½ teaspoon dry mustard powder
½ teaspoon curry powder
½ cup oil, warmed

avocado dip

2 ripe avocados
1 small onion, finely chopped
1 medium tomato, finely chopped
¼ cup sour cream
1 tablespoon lemon juice
Tabasco to taste

Peel and seed avocados, mash flesh well with a fork. Add remaining ingredients to avocado and mix well.

Serve with corn chips, on top of nachos or with Bush-Style Mexican Fajitas, see page

smoked oyster dip

125gm cream cheese
1xtin smoked oysters, drained and chopped
1 teaspoon lemon juice
Black pepper

Combine all ingredients and mx well.

Tip ~ For easy mixing of cream cheese, take it out of the fridge an hour prior to using.

capsicum dip

½ packet of French Onion Soup Mix
300ml carton sour cream
1 teaspoon of chilli powder
2 tablespoons capsicum, finely chopped

Combine all ingredients and mix well.

ham and beer nut dip

½ packet of French Onion Soup Mix
300ml sour cream
½ cup finely chopped ham
¼ cup chopped beer nuts

Combine all ingredients and mix well.

home made salsa

Combine all ingredients.

This salsa is great served as a dip with corn chips and the avocado dip, or can be served with barbecued meat.

Tip ~ If you don't have fresh coriander replace it with 2 teaspoons of minced coriander.

1 red onion, finely chopped
1 tomato, finely chopped
Juice of 1 lemon
2 teaspoons of grated lemon rind
2 tablespoons coriander chopped
½ teaspoon chilli powder

These sweeter nibblies are great served with coffee and/or a port after a great meal - or even at morning and afternoon tea with a cuppa.

the easiest rum balls

Combine all ingredients and mix well. Place in fridge for 10-15 minutes.

Roll into small balls and then cover with extra desiccated coconut.

Makes about 40 balls.

Tip ~ Keep stored in the fridge. These get better after a couple of days!

8 weet bix, crushed
1 cup sweetened condensed milk
2 tablespoons cocoa or drinking chocolate
1 cup desiccated coconut
1 cup chopped dry fruit, try dates, apricots or prunes
¼ cup rum
Extra coconut

nut balls

Combine nuts and biscuits in a bowl.

Combine condensed milk, golden syrup and butter in a saucepan. Place over low heat until melted.

Add condensed milk mixture into nuts and mix well. Make into balls and roll in coconut. Place in fridge until set.

½ cup chopped nuts of your choice
1x250g packet of gingernut biscuits, crushed
¾ cup condensed milk
1 tablespoon golden syrup
2 tablespoons butter
Desiccated coconut

ryan's fav fruit balls

Place fruit into bowl. Pour bowling water over fruit and let stand for 15 minutes.

Add crushed peanuts and skim milk powder and mix well.

Shape into balls and roll in coconut. Place on plate or tray and put in fridge until firm.

Makes about 25 balls.

¾ cup dried fruit, chopped
1 cup sultanas
1 cup dates chopped
½ cup boiling water
½ cup peanuts, crushed
1 cup skim milk powder
½ cup desiccated coconut

MARINADES AND BASTES

Marinades and bastes are great additions for helping create sumptuous meals in your bush kitchen. Why not try one next time you fire up the barbie or camp oven.

marinades

Mix all ingredients in a bowl or screw top jar unless otherwise stated, and then combine with meat and refrigerate for a couple of hours to marinate. Drain meat and reserve marinade/baste to coat meat regularly during cooking.

beef and lamb marinades

marinade 1

2 tablespoons soy sauce

¼ cup oil

2 teaspoons chopped onion

1 teaspoon crushed ginger

marinade 2

¼ cup lemon juice or wine

¼ cup oil

½ teaspoon salt

½ teaspoon pepper

1 garlic clove, crushed

marinade 3

¼ cup oil

1 teaspoon Italian herbs

1 teaspoon grated ginger

2 garlic cloves, crushed

1 tablespoon Worcestershire sauce

½ cup tomato sauce

¼ cup white wine

marinade 4

½ cup red wine

2 tablespoons oil

2 tablespoons soy sauce

2 garlic cloves, crushed

2 tablespoons tomato paste

2 teaspoons Worcestershire sauce

1 tablespoon brown sugar

marinade 5

This one is best used for beef

¾ cup beer

1 tablespoon honey

2 tablespoons brown sugar

1 teaspoon dried mustard

Method
Combine all ingredients in a saucepan and bring to the boil. Simmer for 10 minutes, then cool.

marinade 6

This one is best used for lamb

1 tablespoon ground cumin

1 tablespoon ground coriander

1 teaspoon ground cinnamon

⅓ cup plain yoghurt

Method
Combine all ingredients in a bowl with meat. Refrigerate for 3 hours.

lamb on the spit bastes

baste 1

2 cups lemon juice

1 cup water

1 tablespoon salt

baste 2

2 tablespoons oil

2 tablespoons Worcestershire sauce

½ cup vinegar

½ cup water

¼ cup brown sugar

¼ cup tomato sauce

1 tablespoon tomato paste

baste 3

¼ teaspoon hot English mustard

2 tablespoons white wine

2 tablespoons honey

2 drops of tabasco sauce

1 teaspoon Worcestershire sauce

1 tablespoon lemon juice

½ cup olive oil

Salt and pepper

chicken marinades

marinade 1

1/3 cup honey

1/3 cup oil

2 tablespoons Worcestershire sauce

1 tablespoon grated orange rind

2 garlic cloves, crushed

Great with chicken or fish.

marinade 2

1/2 cup oil

1/4 cup white wine

1 garlic clove, crushed

1/2 teaspoon dried mixed herbs

1 teaspoon minced chilli (or one fresh chilli)

This can be brushed onto chicken, fish or vegetable kebabs.

marinade 3

1/4 cup lemon juice

1/4 cup oil

1/2 teaspoon salt

1 garlic clove, crushed

Pepper to taste

Pineapple juice can be substituted for the lemon juice.

marinade 4

1 tablespoon soy sauce

1/4 cup oil

2 teaspoons chopped onion

1 teaspoon crushed ginger

marinade 5

3 spring onions

2 cloves garlic, crushed

1 cup tomato sauce

4 tablespoons beer

1 tablespoon vinegar

1 tablespoon honey

1 tablespoon tabasco sauce

marinade 6

1/4 cup teriyaki sauce

1/4 cup dry sherry

1 teaspoon crushed ginger

1 teaspoon soft brown sugar

marinade 7

1/2 cup soy sauce

1/3 cup honey

2 teaspoons ground ginger

Combine all ingredients in saucepan and heat through, brush on chicken during cooking.

marinade 8

1 tablespoon curry powder

1/4 teaspoon cinnamon

1/4 teaspoon salt

1/4 cup honey

1 teaspoon soft butter

2 teaspoons lemon juice

1 teaspoon French mustard

Combine the curry powder, cinnamon and salt. Rub into chicken, let rest for 15 minutes. Barbecue or grill chicken brushing with combined honey, butter, juice and mustard.

pork marinades

marinde 1

2 tablespoons olive oil

1 garlic clove, crushed

1 teaspoon chilli powder

1 teaspoon ginger

2 tablespoons soy sauce

2 tablespoons English mustard

2 tablespoons lemon juice

This is great with spare ribs.

marinde 2

3 tablespoons soy sauce

1 tablespoon honey

1 tablespoon brown vinegar

1 teaspoon curry powder

3 tablespoons tomato sauce

1 tablespoon sherry

2 garlic cloves, crushed

1 tablespoon crushed ginger

2 tablespoons sweet chilli sauce

Another great marinade for spare ribs.

marinde 3

4 tablespoons red wine

½ cup honey

¼ teaspoon ground chilli

1 teaspoon mustard powder

This is can be brushed over pork, beef or even sausages.

marinde 4

1 cup pineapple juice

2 tablespoons honey

1 tablespoon soy sauce

2 teaspoons crushed ginger

Combine all ingredients and brush on meat during cooking. This can be used with pork or beef.

seafood marinades

marinde 1

3 tablespoons butter

¼ cup honey

2 teaspoons curry powder

2 teaspoons soy sauce

Heat all ingredients in pan until butter is melted. Brush over barbecued prawns or fish.

marinde 2

3 tablespoons butter

1 teaspoon grated orange rind

⅓ cup orange juice

2 chopped shallots

1 teaspoon crushed ginger

Melt butter in pan and add remaining ingredients. Brush over barbecued prawns, fish or even chicken.

marinde 3

4 tablespoons soy sauce

2 tablespoons honey

2 tablespoons tomato sauce

1 tablespoon grated lemon rind

2 tablespoons sesame seeds (optional)

Combine all ingredients in bowl and add seafood. Marinate in fridge for at least 30 minutes. Great for all prawns, calamari and fish.

CHRISTMAS IN THE BUSH

Glazed ham and roast turkey with all the trimmings and Christmas pudding from your bush kitchen—no worries with these hassle-free recipes for Christmas lunch and dinner in the bush.

Included in this section are a few different recipe ideas for your Christmas lunch or dinner. Instead of carrying a leg of ham or a turkey, which take up quite a bit of room, try the glazed tinned ham or the glazed turkey breasts. And in case there is a total fire ban on Christmas Day, we've included a range of special festive salads that are tasty and filling, as well as easy to prepare. And for afters there is the no fuss Last Minute Christmas Cake and pudding.

glazed ham

Carrying a leg of ham is obviously going to take up some valuable storage space in your car fridge or esky. However, you can still have a glazed ham on Christmas day in the bush. This glazed tinned ham not only takes up little room, but it still looks and tastes great.

Arrange cloves decoratively on top and sides of ham.
Place hams in tray or dish.
Combine glaze ingredients and brush over ham.
Bake in camp oven with coals on bottom and lid for around 30-45 minutes. Baste with glaze a couple of times during cooking.
Bake until glaze is golden and ham is heated through.

Serves 3-4
1x450g can leg or shoulder ham
Whole cloves
Glaze of choice

mustard glaze

2 tablespoons seeded mustard
2 tablespoons honey
1/4 cup orange juice
Mix all ingredients.

apricot glaze

2/3 cup apricot nectar
1/4 cup brown sugar
2 tablespoons honey
1 tablespoon Dijon mustard
Mix all ingredients in a small saucepan and stir over low heat until sugar and honey is dissolved and well mixed.

ginger glaze

1/3 cup honey
1/4 cup chopped glace ginger
1/4 cup brown sugar
1 1/2 tablespoons water
Mix all ingredients in a small saucepan and stir over low heat until sugar and honey is dissolved and well mixed.

roast turkey

The easiest type of turkey to carry is one of the ready to roast rolled turkey breasts or thighs which can be purchased from the supermarket. Remember that these will need to be defrosted for 24-48 hours prior to cooking.

Cook the turkey in a hot camp oven with coals on top of lid for 1 to 2 hours till cooked.

Check regularly to ensure meat is cooking evenly and brush glaze over turkey.

Ready to cook turkey breast or thigh - amount will depend on the number of people to feed

glazed turkey breasts

Serves 4

4 turkey breast fillets
Glaze of choice

Cook turkey breast fillets on lightly oiled barbecue plate or in oiled frying pan, 4-6 minutes each side, brushing with glaze whilst cooking.

orange glaze

2 tablespoons orange marmalade
1 tablespoon orange juice
1 tablespoon mustard powder
1 tablespoon brown sugar

apple glaze

¼ cup apple juice
⅓ cup melted butter
⅓ cup honey

meals for a no — cook christmas

As Christmas is in the height of our fire danger season there are at times a total fire ban on Christmas Day. Therefore we've included some no cook special salads to have on these days. The seafood salads are great for those camping near the coast.

salami and bean salad

Serves 4

125g salami, thinly sliced and cut into strips
1x432g cans red kidney beans, drained and rinsed
1x310g butter beans, drained and rinsed
125g mushrooms, sliced
6 black olives, pitted and sliced
4 shallots, chopped
1 punnet cherry tomatoes, halved

DRESSING
¼ cup olive oil
2 tablespoons red wine vinegar
1 garlic clove, crushed

Combine salami, beans, mushrooms, olives and shallots in a bowl.

Combine all dressing ingredients in a screw top jar and shake well.

Add tomatoes just prior to serving and pour dressing over salad.

prawn salad

Serves 4

Peel prawns and combine with corn, tomatoes, capsicum, avocado and torn lettuce in bowl.

Combine all dressing ingredients and pour over salad.

1kg cooked medium/king prawns

1x440g tin of corn kernels, drained

1 punnet cherry tomatoes, halved

1 capsicum, chopped

1 avocado, sliced

1 lettuce

DRESSING

1 cup mayonnaise

2 tablespoons lemon juice

1 garlic clove, crushed

Few drops of tabasco sauce

prawn and salmon salad

Serves 4

Break salmon into pieces, skin and bones removed.

Combine salmon, prawns, pineapple and capsicum in bowl.

Place lettuce on plates and serve prawn mixture on lettuce.

Combine all dressing ingredients and pour dressing over salad.

500g cooked prawns shelled and deveined, tails intact

1x440g can pineapple pieces, drained

1x220g can red salmon, drained

1 capsicum, sliced

Lettuce

DRESSING

¼ cup mayonnaise

2 tablespoons juice from pineapple

1 tablespoon cream

1 tablespoon tomato sauce

fish salad

Serves 6

2x485g tin of red salmon or tuna
¼ cup lemon juice
4 cucumbers, sliced
1 punnet cherry tomatoes, halved
Lettuce
3 radishes, sliced (optional)
DRESSING
⅓ cup oil
2 tablespoon lemon juice
1 clove garlic crushed

Place well drained fish in bowl with lemon juice, cucumbers, tomatoes and radishes and mix in dressing.

Place lettuce on serving plate and top with fish mixture.

Combine all dressing ingredients in a jar and shake well. Pour dressing over salad.

Tip ~ Be sure to remove skin and bones if using salmon.

chicken & apple salad

Serves 4

1 barbecue chicken
½ red cabbage, shredded
3 apples, cored and sliced
½ cup chopped walnuts
DRESSING
1 ½ cups natural yoghurt
2 teaspoons lemon juice
2 teaspoons of mustard
Salt and pepper to taste

Take all meat off chicken. Combine chicken, cabbage, apples and walnuts in bowl.

Combine all dressing ingredients in a small bowl and mix well. Pour over dressing and mix to coat well.

Tip ~ Use your favourite mustard in the dressing.

last minute christmas pudding

Cream the butter and white sugar. This will take a while doing it by hand, but be persistent.

Dissolve the bicarbonate of soda in the cold tea. Add to tea the creamed butter and sugar, the mixed spice, flour, salt and fruit. Mix well.

Pour mixture into a greased 8 cup pudding basin or dish. Cover with two layers of greaseproof paper and tie. Let stand overnight.

Place pudding basin or dish into camp oven and add enough water to go half way up side of dish. Steam for 2-2½ hours.

Serve with hot custard.

½ cup butter
¾ cup white sugar
2 teaspoons bicarbonate of soda
1 cup cold strong black tea
1 teaspoon mixed spice
4 cups plain flour
Pinch salt
2 cups mixed dried fruit

last minute christmas cake

This is for those of us who may have forgotten all about a Christmas pudding.

Take cake out of packaging and place on a baking tray. Prick cake all over with a skewer.

Cover cake with some foil and heat in a camp oven for about 15 minutes.

Remove from oven and pour ½ cup of chosen liquid over hot cake. When liquid has been absorbed, pour over balance of liquid.

Wait for cake to cool and for all liquid to be absorbed.

Wrap cake in greaseproof paper then foil until ready to serve.

Tip ~ The longer the cake is left the better the flavour.

1 store bought Christmas cake
¾ cup of your choice of either rum, brandy, sherry or apple juice
Foil and greaseproof paper

FAST FOOD

In need of a feed in a hurry, then here are a few ideas
for quick and simple meals while on the go.

Although holidays are about taking it easy, relaxing and enjoying yourself, there are occasions when you'll be pressed for time — this is when you can use a few of the ideas we've listed below to cobble together an enjoyable meal in a matter of minutes.

Hot dogs — Purchase your hot dogs in croyvac packs or in tins. Pull out the gas stove and boil up the hot dogs and place them in some fresh bread, add some grated cheese, sauce and mustard. You can even quickly fry up an onion.

Jaffles — If you're out in the bush, it doesn't take too long to make a small fire to get some hot coals for a toasted jaffle sandwich. You can also use your gas burner. Jaffles always seem to taste best with cheese in them. For savoury fillings try ham, cheese, tomato, onion, tuna, bacon, mushrooms, salami, olives, capsicum, left overs from the night before, pineapple, egg, baked beans, tinned spaghetti, chicken, tinned stews. For sweet filllings try apples sprinkled with sugar, peaches with ground cloves, banana, pineapple. You can also use fruit bread instead of plain bread for a change.

A jaffle iron is a handy addition to your bush cooking kit.

Pan fried sandwiches — If you don't have a jaffle iron or not enough time to make a fire, then pull out the gas stove, a frying pan and an egg flip. Make up your sandwiches, butter the outside of the bread and fry in hot pan on both sides until golden. Good fillings include ham, cheese, tomato, onion, salami.

Wraps — Lavish bread, flour tortillas and pitas are great alternatives to bread, and generally keep longer. Fill with your favourite filling, roll up and enjoy. If you're at camp and have coals, you can also fill these up then wrap them in foil and heat in the camp oven.

From time to time when we're passing through a town around lunch time, we make use of the local park, especially if it has electric or gas BBQs. We'll often grab some fresh bread or rolls, a couple of snags or even a spicy kransky from the local butcher or deli and cook them up with some onion for sausage sangers. Nice and easy and there's no washing up!

section 16

BREWING THE PERFECT CUPPA

The time honoured art of making a cuppa billy tea.

One point to cause a bone of contention around a camp fire must surely be the 'correct' method involved in making the perfect cup of billy tea. It seems no two people can wholeheartedly agree on the best recipe for the bushman's brew.

This aside, there is a time-honoured method that produces the desired results. Give the following a try and see if you too will be converted to billy tea.

Firstly, you need to get the water to a good rolling boil in the billy. Make sure that you use good, clean fresh water. If you are using a new billy for the first time make sure that you get the outside nice and black first. *Never* clean the outside of your billy. Folklore suggests that a green twig placed across the top of the billy while it is on the fire helps reduce the smokey flavour of billy tea. However, I am not convinced of its merit.

Once the water is at a rolling boil and the billy is still on the fire toss your measured amount of tea leaves into the billy. Generally, this would be the amount that would fit in the cup of the palm of your hand or one teaspoon for each person and one for the billy! Some people add a couple of green gum leaves at this point. Try it and see what you think.

Now, the timing is important. You need to let the tea leaves stew for a brief time before removing the billy from the fire. Most reckon about 30 to 45 seconds to

Billy tea - first boil the water then...

be adequate. What happens here is that the tannins from the tea are released by the short boiling process, giving your cuppa its unique taste and colour. If the tea leaves are boiled for too long the resulting cuppa will have a marked bitter taste. Remove the billy from the fire and place on the ground.

The next trick is to settle the tea leaves to the bottom of the billy. The best method is by tapping the side of the billy about half a dozen times with a stick. It's not a good idea to 'swing' the billy in a large arc over your shoulder to help settle the tea leaves. People have ended up with serious scalds from this practice.

Let the billy stand for a minute or two to allow the brew to 'draw', then carefully pour your bush brew into mugs. Purists suggest that billy tea should be drank straight—that is without sugar or milk. But I'll have one of each, thanks. Enjoy.

AUSTRALIAN TERMS

Don't know the difference between a Teamster and a Trapper or a Ringer and a Rouseabout. Then read on!

glossary of terms

A number of old Australian terms have been used throughout this book, here's the low down of their meanings and a few others.

Backblocks — A term that is used to denote a rural area other than the remote, unsettled outback regions.

Baitlayer — Often in drovers camps as a joke, drovers would refer to the cook as a *'baitlayer'*, or in other words his cooking was that bad he was a poisoner.

Beardies — A general term used to describe two bearded bushmen from the New England Region in Northern New South Wales during the 1830s. Subsequently, new squatters to the area were also known as *'Beardies'*. The area bounded by Inverell and Glen Innes is still known today as *'the land of the Beardies'*.

Bullockies — During the early days of settlement some heavy transport and log jinkers where hauled by bullock teams driven by bullock drivers, or *'bullockies'*.

Burdekin Duck — According to *Bill Harney's Cook Book*, *Burdekin Duck* is a bushman's dish made with cold corned beef. Slices of beef were dipped in a batter of flour, baking powder and milk with finely chopped onions and fried in hot dripping until brown.

Bushman's Clock — The laughing kookaburra is commonly known as the *Bushmans Clock*.

Bushman's Hot Dinner — Bill Fern-Wannan in his book *Australian Folklore* describes a bushman's hot dinner as a meal of damper and mustard.

Cobbler — a shearer's term referring to the last sheep left in the pen at the end of a days shearing.

Cocky's Joy — Golden Syrup or Treacle.

Cooee — A far reaching call used in the bush to attract attention.

Damper — A bush bread made from flour and water and baked in the ashes of a camp fire or in a camp oven.

Diamantina Cocktail — A drink originating in Queensland consisting of Bundaberg Rum, condensed milk and an emu's egg.

Digger — The name given to gold miners on the early goldfields. Also refers to Australian soldiers from the first World War.

Dinkum — To be dinkum, or fair dinkum is to be honest, reliable and genuine. The term is said to have arisen from the mispronunciation by a Chinese grog shanty owner of 'fair drinking' in the 1850s.

Doughboy — A boiled flour dumpling.

Drover — A stockman who drives cattle or sheep to market over a long distance, usually in the outback. They commonly used stock routes such as the famous Birdsville Track.

Dungaree Settler — An early Australian small farmer during colonial times who was too poor to wear any other type of clothing except for the faded blue cotton clothes made in India.

Fossicker's Dinner — Consisting of bread, dripping and a roast onion.

Grabben Gullen Pie — According to *Bill Harney's Cook Book*, a Grabben Gullen Pie, or Possum Pumpkin Pie was made from a possum that was cleaned and cut up then roasted in a hollowed out pumpkin until the meat was cooked.

Hargraves — Edward Hammond Hargraves laid claim as the discoverer of gold in Australia at Ophir, New South Wales in 1851. A central west New South Wales village also bears his name.

Hawker — A travelling salesman who often used a horse and wagon to sell his wares which would include everything from pots and pans to lotions and potions.

Jackaroo — The name given to a young man working on a cattle or sheep grazing property to gain experience before becoming an overseer, station manager or moving onto his own place.

Jumbuck — Young lamb.

Mud Pirate — One of a number of terms given to the river boatmen of the Murray-Darling Rivers during the days of paddle-steamers. Others include *inside sailor* and *freshwater seamen*.

Murrumbidgee Jam — A slice of bread dipped in cold tea and sprinkled with sugar—preferably brown sugar.

Never Never — Refers to the far outback.

New Chum — Nineteenth century newly arrived immigrants,

mostly from Britain. New chums were often the butt of practical jokes by old hands.

Overland Trout — A goanna, or any large lizard cooked in the ashes of an open fire were often called overland trout.

Paroo Sandwich — A 'meal' consisting of beer and wine mixed together is known as a Paroo Sandwich.

Ringer — Either a stockman or a champion shearer—usually the 'gun' shearer who shears the highest tally of sheep in the shed over a given period.

Rouseabout — Someone employed as a general hand on a cattle or sheep station.

Shiralee — A type of swag or bedroll and shaped like a leg of mutton. It was carried slung over the shoulder by a strap or piece of rope and was usually balanced by a tucker bag resting on the chest.

Silver City — A name often used for Broken Hill due to its productive lead-zinc mines.

Stockman — Someone who works on a grazing property to handle cattle or sheep.

Stockman's Dinner — A cigarette and a spit make up a Stockman's Dinner.

Sundowner — A swagman who arrived at a property or station late in the afternoon around nightfall when it was too late to work, but he still obtained food and shelter for the night. Sundowners usually left early the next morning.

Swagmen roamed the backblocks in search of work during the depression years of last century.

Swaggie — A man who travelled on foot carrying a swag or bedroll. He survived by doing odd jobs or from handouts. Swaggies were commonplace during the early days of settlement and during the depression years.

Teamster — Another term for Bullockie.

The Black Stump — A mythical landmark that is the border between the settled areas and the remote uninhabited regions. The 'original' black stump lies just to the north of the central western New South Wales town of Coolah.

Underground Mutton — A term used for rabbits.

supplier listing

The cooking gear featured throughout this book is all top quality, Australian made equipment that with care will last for many years. It is available from camping and outdoor stores or by mail order from the manufacturer.

Auspit
Rhett Thompson
PMT Leisure Pty Ltd
PO Box 451, Pakenham Vic 3810
Phone: (03) 5941 3949
Web: www.pmtleisure.com.au/auspit.html

Aussie Porta Spits
Darren Brooks
PO Box 23, Hackham SA 5163
Phone: (08) 8327 3559 Fax: (08) 8327 4466
Mobile: 0417 089 091
Web: www.aussieportaspits.com.au

Bedourie Camp Ovens
Southern Metal Spinners
2 Piping Lane, Lonsdale, South Australia 5160
Phone: (08) 8382 6990 Fax: (08) 8326 1369
Email: sales@southernmetalspinners.com.au
Web: www.southernmetalspinners.com.au

Biji Barbi
Tony Upton
PO Box 110, Hillston NSW 2675
Phone/Fax: (02) 6967 2417

Carr-B-Que
John E Carr
PO Box H142, Hurlstone Park NSW 2193
Phone: (02) 9558 5447
Mobile: 0417 921 347

Eco Billy
Kym Crowhurst
Murray River Innovations Pty Ltd
PO Box 644, Berri SA 5343
Phone/Fax: (08) 8582 2441
Mobile: 0428 822 441
Email: kcrowmri@riverland.net.au

Furphy Foundry
PO Box 1912, Shepparton Vic 3630
Phone: (03) 5831 2777 Fax: (03) 5831 2681
Email: furphy@mcmedia.com.au
Web: www.furphyfoundry.com.au

Hillbilly Camping Gear
Mick Mills
23 Mt Morton Rd, Belgrave South Vic 3160
Phone/Fax: (03) 9754 5053
Email: hillbilly@bluep.com
Web: www.campingwithhillbilly.com

Nipper Kipper Smoke Ovens
Trevor Dixon
73 Karraschs Road, Craignish Qld 4655
Phone: (07) 4128 6491 Fax: (07) 4128 6381
Email: cooking@smokeovens.com
Web: www.smokeovens.com

Togar Ovens
Graham Joshua
PO Box 660, Beenleigh Qld 4207
Phone/Fax: (07) 5546 4347
Mobile: 0438 452 414
Email: info@togarovens.com
Web: www.togarovens.com

index

Other Great Titles from Boiling Billy Publications

CAMPING GUIDEBOOKS

Camping Guide to New South Wales. This guide contains detailed information on over 570 camp sites in 237 national parks, state forests, state parks and riverside reserves throughout New South Wales. Includes caravan access, dog friendly sites and much more for the avid camper.

Camping Guide to Victoria. With this guide in hand you will be able to find that perfect camp site in one of the 206 parks, forests and reserves listed in Victoria. This guide also includes detailed information on vehicle access, dog friendly sites and much more on 550 sites.

Camping Guide to South Australia. This guide contains details on camping areas within national parks, state forests, conservation parks and public reserves throughout South Australia, including the popular Flinders Ranges, the outback areas and Murray River forests.

Camping Guide to the Northern Territory. Details camping areas within national parks, conservation parks and public reserves throughout the Northern Territory including all the major destinations.

Camping Guide to Tasmania. This best selling guide details camping areas within national parks, state forests, state parks and public reserves throughout Tasmania, including the stunning east coast, the central lakes district and the rugged west coast. Includes dog friendly locations.

Camping Guide to Western Australia. Details camping areas within national parks, state forests, conservation parks and council reserves throughout Western Australia. Includes the popular Kimberley and Pilbara regions and the south-west forests. Also includes caravan access and dog friendly sites.

Camping Guide to Queensland. This comprehensive guide details camping areas within national parks, state forests, conservation parks and council reserves throughout Queensland. Includes many little known camp sites as well as dog friendly destinations.

FOUR-WHEEL DRIVE GUIDES

4WD Treks Close to Sydney – Fourth Edition. A completely revised and updated expanded edition covering old favourites plus new tracks within a couple of hours drive from Sydney. Features new full page maps as well as lat/long and UTM GPS readings.

4WD Tracks of the High Country. Discover 20 of the best 4WD destinations in Australia's magical high country. Each destination is fully route noted with GPS readings as well as detailed information on track conditions, maps and camping opportunities.

4WD Treks Close to Melbourne – Second Edition. A completely revised and updated expanded edition detailing old favourites plus many new tracks within a couple of hours drive from Melbourne. Features new full page maps as well as lat/long and UTM GPS readings.

4WD Touring New South Wales. A collection of route directed touring treks taking in outback rivers, long forgotten gold mining towns, stunning national parks, winding mountain tracks and enjoyable beach runs — and even a few of New South Wales's colourful bush pubs. Readers can explore a selection of the state's best 4WD destinations along with some of its facinating history.

4WD Touring South East New South Wales and East Gippsland. 20 four-wheel drive tours in the region straddling the New South Wales/Victorian border. Features full page maps as well as lat/long and UTM GPS readings.

w w w . b o i l i n g b i l l y . c o m . a u

a great mate for the great outdoors...